edge walking on the western rim

new works by 12 northwest writers

Sherman Alexie

Sharon Doubiago

David James Duncan

Sam Hamill

Lawson Fusao Inada

Colleen J. McElroy

Brenda Peterson

Jonathan Raban

Tom Robbins

Charlotte Watson Sherman

Tom Spanbauer

William Stafford and Kim R. Stafford

edge walking on the western rim

new works by 12 northwest writers

Photographs by Bob Peterson

Edited and with profiles by Mayumi Tsutakawa

Printed in Hong Kong
First edition

The New Works by 12 Northwest Writers reading series and this resulting collection of work
were made possible with generous support from the Lila Wallace–Reader's Digest Fund.

Some of the information in the William Stafford profile was adapted from the educational
documentary videotapes *What the River Says* (1989) and *The Life of the Poem* (1992), and their
accompanying material, by producers Vince Wixon and Michael Markee, Ashland, Oregon.

The William Stafford poems "Sniffing the Region" and "Forestry" are reprinted with permission
of Confluence Press. The poems "Night in Oregon," "Everyone Out Here Knows," and "Want List"
are reprinted with permission of Adrienne Lee Press. The poem "Lake Chelan" is reprinted with
permission of the William Stafford estate.

Portions of "Beluga Baby: An Afterlife of Animals" by Brenda Peterson appeared in the November/
December 1993 issue of *New Age Journal*.

"My Life as a Screamer," by Judith Roche, is included in her book of poems *Myrrh/My Life as a
Screamer*, published by Black Heron Press, 1993.

The text of this book is composed in Joanna and Gill Sans
Manufacturing by C & C Offset Printing, Hong Kong

Book design by Katy Homans and Deborah Zeidenberg

ISBN 1-57061-013-4

LIBRARY OF CONGRESS CATALOGING-IN-PUBLICATION DATA
Edge walking on the western rim : new works / by 12
Northwest writers ; photographs by Bob Peterson : edited and
with profiles by Mayumi Tsutakawa.
p.   cm.
ISBN 1-57061-013-4 : $19.95
1. American literature—Northwestern States. 2. American
literature—Northwestern States—History and criticism—Theory,
etc. 3. Northwestern States—Literary collections. I. Peterson,
Bob. 1941-   . II. Tsutakawa, Mayumi.
PS570.E34 1994   94-9138
810.9'9795—dc20   CIP

Co-published by One Reel and Sasquatch Books
Distributed by Sasquatch Books
1008 Western Avenue
Suite 300
Seattle, WA 98104
206.467.4300

Contents

Foreword

Shawn Wong

So this New York cabbie from Egypt asks me, "What's Seattle like?" It's been a long flight, I'm tired, and I don't want to get into a long discussion, so I pass over the categories about rain, mountains, salmon, and coffee. I say, "No one honks their horn. Pedestrians don't jaywalk. You can turn right on a red light." The Egyptian cabbie looks at me in the rearview mirror and laughs. He repeats what I said like a poem:

> No one honks their horn.
> Pedestrians don't jaywalk.
> You can turn right on a red light.

He laughs again and, I think out of gratitude for giving him the above Northwest mantra, takes me the cheap way from La Guardia to midtown Manhattan without asking.

The next day I'm attending the American Booksellers Association convention and I'm lost inside the Jacob Javits Convention Center. An older man sees me studying my map of the building and asks if he can help. As I tell him the room number I'm looking for, I look down at his name tag and it reads, "William Stafford/Author." The only poem I know by heart is Stafford's "Traveling Through the Dark." Before I can introduce myself, he says, "I've just come from that room, I'll walk you over there." Bill Stafford, poet, shows me the way.

Stafford's work concludes the *edge walking on the western rim* collection. The authors and poets assembled here are certainly not meant to be the definitive Northwest writers (otherwise they would all be wearing plaid shirts, eating salmon, and drinking coffee in their photos). However, their inclusion in the book allows us to share their diverse sense of place and literary vision of this Northwest landscape.

I know a few of the writers in this book and had read almost all of them before their arrival on these pages. Colleen McElroy and I have talked about our Chinese ancestors. Lawson Inada and I have driven together over the southern Oregon border to visit the site of the Japanese-American concentration camp at Tule Lake. Tom Robbins and I have shared Chinese banquets in Seattle's International District. Perhaps our literary act of belonging here is as simple as this—food, ancestry, and place.

I was recently reminded that this anthology was my idea; I also remember declining to edit it. I didn't want to work on the project; I just wanted to see what would happen. When given the chance, what would twelve Northwest writers say about the place they call home, the place where their writing begins? That question is answered a dozen times in the pages that follow. In these writings the landscape of the Northwest meets the literary landscape of the imagination. *edge walking*.

Introduction

Mayumi Tsutakawa

Terra firma sang the feet
deep in warm sand.
shi shi beach
shi shi, the sand sang back, shi shi
shi shi
edge walking on the western rim.

—from "My Life as a Screamer" by Judith Roche

edge walking on the western rim is not just a literary anthology. From its inception, the idea has been to create more than a collection of new essays by widely recognized writers who have chosen to live and work in Washington and Oregon. We also wanted to make this body of works into a visually creative documentary through the extensive use of photographs. We added personal profiles to shed further light on the writers' lives in order to present a richer, multidimensional look at the writers.

The group of twelve writers (really thirteen with the combination of work by William Stafford and Kim R. Stafford) was asked to submit an essay or group of poems on the theme of "place." In the work, they were to reflect on their choice of the Northwest as a home for living and working—the natural or cultural atmosphere they seek, the draw of a native place or families, the blessed (or damned) isolation from urban centers of power elsewhere.

With Shawn Wong (writer and University of Washington professor), Rick Simonson (coordinator of readings at Elliott Bay Book Company), and Judith Roche (poet and One Reel literary organizer), I worked to choose writers of diverse style, gender, geography, ethnicity, birthplace, and literary genre. In the course of organizing the book, we stretched our boundaries to include not only some writers fairly new to the Northwest (Jonathan Raban, for example), but also some whose lives are bound by their long-time Northwest homes, although they have moved a little farther away (as with Portland native David James Duncan or the nomadic Sharon Doubiago). Likewise, we found Northwest writers who travel a lot (such as Colleen J. McElroy) making important statements about the need to return to the comfort of their cool, rainy home.

Some of these writers found that, to write about living here, they had to call upon ancient histories or the memories of those who lived here before. For others, the sources were family matters or personal decisions. Some found the process excruciating, some joyful. The writers argue that we live in language rather than in physical place. The variety and dynamism of the anthology is precisely in this mix, reflecting a Northwest of many artists and many peoples yet unified by attention to a natural setting that reaches from rough ocean currents to forested (or clearcut) peaks to vast desert.

I feel privileged to have had the opportunity to work on this project. A native of Seattle (my father also was born in Seattle, in 1910), I deeply believe that the choice to live and work in the Northwest is not only a wise and healthy one, but one that affords us a wide range of natural *and* cultural options. We see high mountains an hour to the east and saltwater inlets at our doorstep. We have close proximity to the Pacific Rim nations. A growing economy and rapidly changing demographics of our region promise continuous cultural learning and interesting community living, both urban and rural.

We hope we have captured a range of thought, representative of the many writers whose inner voices have compelled them to live and write on the western edge of our country.

I wish to thank Louise DiLenge of One Reel for her unstinting (and unstoppable) work as chief organizer of this anthology project, as well as Anne Depue of Sasquatch Books for her fine editing advice. Without these two people, the project would not have come to fruition.

January 1994

River Teeth

David James Duncan

When an ancient streamside conifer is finally washed or blown from
its riverbank to crash down into the water, a complex disintegration
process begins. The fallen tree becomes a naked log; the log begins to
lead a kind of afterlife in the river; and this afterlife is, in some ways,
of greater benefit to the river than was the original life of the tree.

A living tree stabilizes riverbanks, helps cool water temperatures,
provides shade and cover for fish, shelter for mammals, perches for
kingfishers, and so on. But fallen trees serve some of these same pur-
poses, and other crucial ones besides. The gradual disintegration of a
log in a streambed creates, for example, a vast transfusion of nutrients—a slow forest-to-river feast reaching from the saprophytic bottom
of the food chain to the predatory, fly-casting, metaphor-making top.
Dead trees are also part of a river's filtration system: working in concert
in logjams, they become flotsam traps; mud, leaf, and carcass traps; Sty-
rofoam, disposable diaper, monofilament, and beer-can traps. Downed
trees are also a key element in river hydraulics: a log will either force
current *down*, thus digging a sheltering pocket, and maybe a gravel bed
suitable for spawning; or *around*, thus digging an undercut bank; or at
the very least *over*, creating a white-water spill that pumps life-giving
oxygen into the stream.

On the forest streams I know best—those of the Oregon Coast
Range clearcuts, "tree farms," and token strips of rain forest—the
breakdown of an old-growth river log takes only a couple of decades.
Tough as logs are, the grinding of sand, water, and ice are relentless,
ultraviolet light speeds breakdown, and the seasonal wet/dry, wet/dry
pattern attacks the wood, too. Within a half decade or so, any drowned
conifer but cedar turns punk, grows waterlogged, and joins the rocks
and crayfish as features of the river's bottom. And even after burial,
decomposition continues. The log breaks into filaments, the filaments
become gray mush, the mush becomes mud, washes down river,
comes to rest in side channels. The side channels fill, and gradually
close. New trees spout from the muck. The cycle goes on.

There are, however, parts of every dead tree that seem to refuse
to become part of the cycle. There is, in every log, a series of cross-
grained, pitch-hardened masses where long-lost branches once joined
the tree's trunk. "Knots," they're called in a piece of lumber. But in the
bed of a river, after the parent log has broken down and vanished, these
stubborn masses take on a very different appearance, and so perhaps
deserve a different name. "River teeth" is what we called them as kids
—because that's what they looked like. Like enormous fangs, really,
with a connected cross-grained root. They even turn a toothy white if
you dry them. It took me a while to realize, when I found my first,
that it had once been a part of a tree. Having grown up around talk of

"headwaters" and "river mouths," it was easier for me to imagine it having washed loose from some sort of literal river's jaw than having once joined a branch to an evergreen.

In hand, a river tooth feels bronze-hard, bronze-heavy, and weapon-like. A blow from the blunt end or stab from the fang could kill. The flood-driven sands and stones never quit grinding at them, but grinding only seems to sharpen their points. I don't know just how long the bigger ones last, but even on the rainy coast I'd guess centuries: you sense antiquity when you heft one. Because their pitch content is so high, and because hardened pitch outlasts the grainy wood fiber, the oldest teeth lose their resemblance to trees or driftwood and begin to look more like tools, or even art objects—something intelligently worked, not just worn. And to an extent I feel that this is what they become. There is life in rivers, and strength; there are countless stone tools; in a relic the waters have shaped so long, why wouldn't we begin to glimpse the river's mind and blind artistry as well?

♦

With my trees, logs, and river in place, I'd like to piece together a metaphor:

Our present-tense human experience, our lives in the inescapable present, are like living trees. Our memories of experience, our individual pasts, are like trees fallen in a river. The current in that river is the passing of time. And a story—a good shared story—is the transfusion of nutrients from the old river log of memory into the eternal now of life.

But as the current of time keeps flowing, the aging log begins breaking down. Once-vivid impressions begin to rot. Years run together. Dates of key events vanish. We try to share, with an old friend or spouse, some "memorable" past experience, and end up arguing instead about details misconstrued. Chunks of the log begin to vanish completely. Someone approaches us in a crowd, their face lights up, they say their name, tell us of some past connection—and we shake their hand and grin through our horror, unable to place them at all. Some of us realize, after being endlessly corrected, that there are portions of our pasts we can no longer weave into accurate narratives at all. Others of us realize, after sharing the same accurate narrative for decades, that we have somehow talked our allotment of stories to death, that no one's listening any longer, that when we speak our old stories the room fills with a dark water and our listeners' eyes roll or glaze. So we stop telling the stories. We let them decompose. The last filaments of memory become gray mush, the mush becomes mud, the mud washes downriver. New life, and new stories, sprout up in the fertile silence. The cycle goes on.

There are, however, small parts of every human past that resist this natural cycle; there are hard, cross-grained whorls of memory that remain inexplicably lodged in us long after the straight-grained narratives have washed away. Most of these whorls are not stories, exactly; more often they're just self-contained moments of shock, or of inordinate empathy; moments of violence, incomprehension, surreality; moments of lust, tomfoolery, uncaught dishonesty; mystical terror; joy. These are our "river tooth" experiences. They are what remains in us after the rest of our autobiographies are gone.

True river tooth experiences are always old; until the narrative fiber that surrounds them turns punk and vanishes, one can't be sure they possess the adamantine quality that is their chief attribute. They are also fairly brief—just as actual wooden river teeth are fairly small. In most of my own such experiences I have been more acted upon than actor, more eye than body, more witness than hero. Yet their emotional impact is always strong, and their emotional range is vast. Some of the hardest, if told to the wrong person, would certainly wound, and could perhaps even kill. Yet others, though equally hard, possess the solidity of a geographer's bearing marker, and help us find our way.

Almost everyone, I believe, owns scores of these old knots and whorls, and yet I hear very few people speak of them. My hope, in displaying a few personal river teeth here, is to make others more aware of their own.

RED COATS

It's a few days before Christmas, downtown Portland. I am three years old. My mother, two brothers, sister, and I have come in from the country by bus. We're here to shop and, I guess, meet Santa Claus. But I'm not interested in Santa. I'm interested in survival. The doors of every car, trolley, bus, and building in town are extruding humans, most of them traveling at a pace that equals my dead run, all of them bigger, some ten times bigger, than me. The air at my face level is so thick with scissoring thighs, swinging purses, and jingling trouser-pockets that I can't risk even glancing at the window displays. My brother John is seven, and nearly competent to handle this chaos. But Steve is four and incompetent, so John is under orders to hold his hand and walk directly in front of my mother, whose arms and attention are occupied with a purse, four or five shopping bags, a Christmas list, and my baby sister. That leaves me to bring up the rear—and I am under orders to maintain my position by clinging to my mother's bright red winter coat.

I am, fervently, clinging. I know that only by obedience will I survive. We've already walked dozens of blocks, entered revolving or swinging or sliding double doors, traversed the aisle-mazes of boiling hot buildings, ridden fang-stepped escalators and airless, fart-filled elevators only to shoot, sweating and dizzy, back out into the cram-packed cold. As we head for the Meier & Frank building and our rendezvous with Santa, the sidewalk is so thick with percussing shoes that I can scarcely see concrete. One misstep by one of the thousand spiked heels and my foot could end up looking like the foot of Our Lord. On a mid-block sidewalk Mom escapes a knot of people by angling us over to the edge of the street—and a delivery truck nearly mows us down. At a crosswalk, moments later, she swims us off the curb in the midst of the human current, sees the DON'T WALK sign flash, slams into reverse, smacks her red wool bottom into my face, crushes my head into the keys of some fat guy's pockets, changes her mind, hollers "Run!," and I am barely able to catch the salvific red coat and follow it, dazed, back into the current.

The coat is trolling me now, like a half-drowned herring, through a crush of silhouettes along the shadowed side of a building. The people across the street, in contrast, look ablaze in the winter sunlight. Despite my sensory overload I am fascinated by their brilliance. It fascinates me, too, to see a woman among them in a blazing red coat who looks a lot like my mother. Tightening my grip on my real mother's coat, I see that the sunlit mother is even carrying a baby. And right in front of her are two boys dressed a lot like my brothers. Funny. The only thing misssing is the boy dressed like me. I tug on Mom's coat, wanting to show her our near-twin family. She feels the tug, turns, gives me a surprised little smile—

and something's happened to her face. It's wrong, wrong! Every piece of it, lips, eyes, nostrils, is different; not ugly, not bad, just hopelessly different. Hoping it's some trick of the shadows, or of makeup, I gasp, "What did you *do?*"

She just stares down at me, then laughs—a strange, nervous titter— and in a strange voice says, "You're holding my coat."

Of course I am. And I keep holding it. But she's lost the baby, she's lost my brothers, she's lost her face. Does she want me to let go so she can lose me now, too? Too scared to confront her violent foreignness, I look for the family I'd wanted to show her. There they are, in the beautiful blazing light. And look. The red-coated mother just noticed me here in the shadows. Noticed me, then gaped, then looked behind her. Now she's pointing me out to her boys. They gape, too. The woman and boys start waving and shouting. The Steve-like one starts jumping. The John-like one starts laughing. Even the baby is waving. And I can't understand them, it's way too noisy, but they're acting as if they know me, acting as if they want me. And though I feel it's a betrayal, I suddenly want them, too.

So I drop the red coat. I let it fall, turn toward the sunlit family, bolt right into the street. But when she sees me coming the sunlit mother screams, tires scream, pavement screams, I feel violent hands, engine heat, my body flying backwards, the wind of a speeding car—

and I'm back in the shadows, in my weird-faced mother's arms. But she is squeezing me now, she is holding me tight. And strange as she still looks, I know she has just saved my life.

I give her a tentative hug. She smiles an odd smile in response. But she doesn't laugh or titter. She looks scared now—as scared as me. And even scared her face is pretty, maybe prettier than before. I don't know what she did with my brothers or baby sister, but I know by the way she's holding me that they must be okay. "Just wait," she tells me in her quiet new voice—and I like the voice, too. "I'll wait with you. Don't worry. They're coming. See?"

Following the line of her long, elegant finger, I see the sunlit mother herding her boys and baby toward the corner crosswalk. But now I don't understand. I love my changed red-coated mother despite her sudden difference. And the whole time she holds me, the whole time I wait, I believe that I'm about to change families.

ROSE VEGETABLES

In 1960, on one of the hottest June days on record, I went with my family to watch the Grand Floral Parade of Portland's annual Rose Festival. "Rose Vegetable," hippie friends would later dub it, with no argument from me. At age eight, though, one assumes, when a billion flowers get beheaded and thrust on public display, that they've died for some noble purpose. So there I hunched, front-row-seated on the curb, watching the edible-looking floats and neurotic clowns, the gymnasts, marching bands and National Guard rockets, the sequined majorettes, stunt men and stilt men, unicyclists, Indian chiefs, rope-trick artists. White-gloved, admiration-stoned princesses reached toward us through the air, slowly unscrewing invisible jar lids. Beefy Rosarians glad-handed us. Rows of robotic soldiers disdained us. Snack and toy vendors hustled and fed us. Magicians and jugglers regaled us. And none of them stuck around long enough to bore us. I grew mesmerized. I can't say for sure that I was having fun, but I was definitely an enthralled little Rose Vegetable, pleased as Pepsi to be a Portlander, wishing I'd a flag, gun, or red rose to wave.

The Meadowland Dairy wagon came clomping toward us—a huge, turn-of-the-century bandwagon drawn by eight enormous black Clydesdales, with a uniformed brass band aboard. The parade abruptly halted, in that inexplicable way parades do, placing the wagon right in front of us. The band lit into some better-than-average Sousa. Parade-goers began bobbing to it like hundreds of happy toilet plungers. Then, without warning, one of the Clydesdales spooked, shrieked, tried to rear in its traces. All seven of the other horses began doing the same. The brass band was jerked so violently the Sousa stopped cold. And it was suddenly obvious, as the wagon driver roared his puny *Whoas* and jerked futile reins, and mothers began gripping kids, that those horses could drag the wagon anywhere they chose, including straight through the marching band in front of them, or into the crowd on either side.

That was when I first noticed the man who'd been trudging along by the Clydesdales from the beginning. Just this bland-faced, pale old bald guy, wearing black slacks and a short-sleeved shirt so boring he looked more like a lost salesman than a part of a gala parade. Definitely not the guy you'd choose to save the day. But he was holding a riding crop in one hand. And he shuffled back along the rearing team, applied his crop to the trouble horse, and managed, in no time, to quell all eight of them. And no sooner had he done this than he fell face down on the asphalt. And didn't move, though the pavement was blistering hot. Seeing this odd behavior, the horses took a few nervous steps forward, and the wagon's huge wooden-spoked, steel-rimmed wheels turned just once. But once was enough: while we stared as if at another clown stunt or magician's trick, the right front wheel of the Meadowland Dairy wagon rolled, with majestic slowness, not so much over as *through* the old man's head . . .

The smell of a hospital, the air in a full church—these are all it normally takes to make me faint. But the sense of unreality the parade had engendered in me was so profound that not even the sound of crunching skull, not even the spilt and bloodied gray brain made me queasy. When easily twenty-five people, including my father, suddenly flopped to the ground as if playing Simon Says with the dead man, the unreality only thickened; I didn't understand till my father recovered and told me that it had been a mass faint.

It betrays my slant on civic pride that I consider this, by far, the most edifying Rose Festival event I've ever witnessed. When I try to this day to grasp the driving force behind words like Karma, Destiny, or Fate, I picture those eight enormous black Clydesdales. And when I first read of the Buddhist symbol of the Great Wheel, you can imagine which wheel's slow turning sprang to mind.

So, what a comedown, what a piffle-ization, the next morning, to watch my parents paw the daily *Oregonian* from end to end and find that the only mention of this soul-shaking event was a three-sentence piece of denial on the obituary page. The old guy had died a hero; he'd gone down for the Rose Vegetable cause. He was the first thing I'd seen outside a boob tube or movie theater that bore resemblance to a legitimate Victim Savior. And the paper stated his name, age, and ex-address, stated the time and place of his death, called the cause of his death "heatstroke," and that was that.

The Lord can only giveth. The media account is free to sweep what the Lord giveth away. This was my first exposure to this gruesome kind of cleanup operation. I have distrusted newspapers and civic celebrations ever since. But I have also believed, ever since, that we still live among quiet heroes.

A STREET LAMP IN THE NETHERLANDS

Early August 1969. I was standing on a sidewalk outside a delftware factory in Amsterdam, smoking an English Pall Mall cigarette. The sun was bright, the morning still, the neighborhood old, the houses stately, and the dullness of the delftware lecture my teenage American traveling companions were enduring indoors added to the pleasure of my smoke. It was a two-lane, one-way street, evenly lined with broadleaf trees and enormous old wrought-iron street lamps. They were the sort of street lamps—we'd seen them all over Europe—that had been converted, decades ago, from gas to electricity. They'd been standing for close to a century. They had survived two world wars. And as I was staring up the empty street, my head equally empty but for a nicotine buzz, a lamp a hundred or so feet away let out a groan, then fell with a crash to the pavement.

As soon as it happened I looked in every direction to see if anyone else had witnessed its fall. The only person in sight was a silhouette in the back seat of a Fiat sedan, parked across the street from the delftware factory. The Fiat's windows were closed; the person seemed not to have noticed. I was disappointed. A fellow witness and I could have shared an amazed laugh. Alone, I was having trouble believing what I'd seen. Yet there the lamp lay, blocking half the street, its glass panes shattered, its post badly twisted. "Weird," I said aloud.

Hearing a buzzing sound, I looked past the fallen lamp and saw a Vespa motor scooter. As it came closer I could make out a neatly dressed young man in front, and a pair of bare knees just behind him. Closer yet the knees began to shine in the morning light. Closer yet I saw that they belonged to a pretty young woman, and that the miniskirt she was wearing was forced, by the wind and her posture, clear up to her panties. Confused though I was by the street lamp, I was smitten with lust by the way her beautiful bare legs embraced the young man.

They'd been using the right lane. When the man saw the fallen lamp he swerved, scarcely slowing, to the left lane. Neither he nor the woman showed any surprise at the sight of the lamp. As they passed me, doing perhaps twenty-five, I felt myself staring so carnivorously at her exposed legs that I attempted a friendly wave in hopes of softening, somewhat, my wretched manners. The young man ignored me, and the woman didn't wave, either, but she flashed me a marvelous smile. Doubly smitten, I was still staring at her receding legs when the silhouette in the Fiat at the left curb suddenly opened the door. The couple on the Vespa had no time to react. The door missed the young man, but struck the woman in the center of the kneecap. Her leg snapped violently backwards, the scooter was turned sideways, but the young man, using his feet as struts, somehow brought it to an upright stop. The woman slumped to the pavement and began to let out horrible, gasping groans. The person in the Fiat remained frozen in the backseat, gaping at them both.

They were surrounded within seconds by people from the delftware factory. I tried to go to them, too. But when I saw the dent her knee had made in the metal edge of the car door, saw shattered bone knifing and blood spilling from the beautiful tan of her leg, I found myself veering like a drunk back to the curb I'd started from, the blood gone from my head. And as I hunched like a gargoyle on my curb there, trapped between the remembered gleam of her legs and the animal agony of her groans, I kept looking up the street at the preposterously fallen lamp that started the chain reaction, trying endlessly, like a gargoyle, to work out a way to hate it; to think of a way to make it pay.

GIVING NORMAL THE FINGER
(FOR KATHERINE DUNN)

When I was eight I had a foster brother, also eight, whom I'll call Edward. This Edward had brown hair, green eyes, a gravelly voice, a muscular torso, and a huge, irresistible laugh. What he didn't have was arms and legs. Not even stumps. Just a single finger, complete with joints and a normal nail, growing straight out of his right shoulder. For some reason it always struck me as an index finger.

Thalidomide did it. People said this confidently, as if that took care of that. But the word thalidomide did no more to change Edward's experience of being Edward than the Platonic myth about men and women having once been eight-limbed, single-bodied hermaphrodites has done to change my experience of being a four-limbed, mono-gendered male. We've all been severed from something. The older we get, the more numerous and beloved this something gets. The name for this process, I believe, is Life. And Edward's company was great early exposure, for my siblings and me, to the beautiful harsh flow of it.

The Eddie we knew was tone-deaf, loved to sing at the top of his lungs anyhow, and could select sing-along records and slap 'em on the turntable with just his finger, cheek, and mouth. His other great love was for what he called "wrassling," which consisted of chasing us, mostly, by wobbling along on his base like a penguin while we walked along in front of him begging him to give up. But he never did give up. And when we finally gave in and let him catch us by an arm with his chin and shoulder, he would—I'm not joking—either flip us hard, right over his back, or nearly jerk our arms out trying. It was a little emasculating to hear my mother telling this limbless, two-and-a-half-foot-tall phenom not to be so rough with her able-bodied boys. But Edward of course loved these admonitions. And, laugh if you like, he was scary; he had a full-bore heart, full-sized willpower, and no extremities to slow any part of it down. Eddie was *condensed*, and he cherished his greater density. It gave him greater intensity, and he knew it. In fact, the bane of his existence, in his own fierce opinion, was the physical therapists who wanted to teach him the use of artificial arms and legs, and so disperse that intensity. Adults, including my parents, were flabbergasted by his hatred of prosthetics. But put yourself in Eddie's shoes. Edward. Shoes. Get the picture? Have a friend tie your feet to your butt and your arms to your chest, stack two chairs, lift you onto the top chair, then knock you over with only one finger free to break your fall. Get the picture? We were instructed by our parents to praise Eddie when he used a steel "arm" that was actually a claw to accidentally scratch, chip, and ruin the records he could easily play without it. This industrial claw, the experts said, would help him lead a "more normal life." But Eddie sought a balance he could live with. Like Artie Binewski, the great twisted hero of Katherine Dunn's *Geek Love*, Eddie seemed to feel that a boy geeked in body was best off geeked at heart as well. The only "normality" he therefore sought was to be self-sufficient, loved if possible, and generally accepted by humans for being just the way God made him. And if it wasn't God—if it was industrial man and thalidomide that made him—so much the more reason why industrial humans should accept him as he was.

My family gave it a go. After a year of monthly visits we tried a straight two-week stint of Edward's company. And when it was over we decided it felt workable, that to take him in was something we were willing to do. The only gray area, for me, was a Huck and Jim–type moral quandary: the first thing Edward always did behind closed doors was swear me to secrecy, then have me unstrap the hated steel arm.

In December, a year after we'd met him, we were finally allowed to talk openly with Eddie about the possibility of adoption; to ask, for instance—though it seemed to me to go without asking—whether *he* wanted *us*. His response baffled us all. He seemed superficially flattered, yet essentially indifferent. But when I thought twice about it, I began to understand: whereas I saw my siblings as great companions and playmates and my parents as kind and wise, Eddie saw four fleet-footed kids who'd grown increasingly sick of "wrassling" with him, and a pair of adults who believed in plastic legs and steel claws.

The adoption question was unexpectedly resolved when someone beat us to it—a "good Christian family," as the adoption people put it, with a farm in the country, and a house big enough for Eddie to get a room of his own. When the good Christian wife heard about us from our near-miss brother, she sent a letter saying how blessed they were to have him, and included an article and photograph from their local paper. In the photo the family, Eddie now among them, stood on the steps of the institution that had housed him for years, all of them smiling and all "heading home." But since it was a cold December day and the kids were all in coats, hats, boots, and mittens, you couldn't even tell, from the picture, which kid was wearing four prosthetics as well. The effect was visually tranquilizing. What thalidomide had done, a therapist and photographer had temporarily undone. Yet one member of the family was risking his life in order to teeter there, grinning, at the brink of those concrete stairs.

◆

We heard rumors, during my and Edward's teens, that his life with the farm family had blown up: rumors of alcohol and drugs, of trouble with the law, of multiple disappearances—all things that could also have been said of me. We heard his adoptive family had finally refused to have anything more to do with him. Then we heard nothing. But a decade and a half later, when I was twenty-two years old, I saw a guy I knew could only be Eddie working his penguin-like way along a sidewalk near the Portland State University campus.

He was wearing a pair of gray gym shorts, some kind of padding at the base of his pelvis, and that was it. His torso was still incredibly muscular, but beyond tan or leather: he was scraped and worn as an old punching bag. The one finger was thick and strong, like that of a construction worker. His fingernail was dirty. His voice, disarmingly rusty in childhood, now sounded like a gregarious piece of road-paving equipment. But it was his face that really struck me. It had a kind of apoplectic ruddiness about it, looked easily thirty-five, and after one look at his eyes I knew that his great intensity had been burning him up all these years, that it would continue to burn him up until he was ashes, and that there was nothing anyone could do to change this. The heart is designed to shoot life and energy clear out to the extremities: in Eddie's eyes at age twenty-two you saw his heart, life, and energy crashing against a wall, trying to invent extremities.

I introduced myself, described our past connection, but felt some doubt about whether he remembered me. When I offered him a cigarette, though—a hand-rolled Three Castles—he had no objection to giving me an update on his life. We walked over to the library lawn and sat, or I did; sitting and standing were identical postures for him. Then he talked, disjointedly but intensely, and also proudly, of obstacles he'd faced and of things he'd done. He was, I felt, perfectly honest. He'd been honest at eight; he seemed no different now. There was nothing self-aggrandizing about his stories, nothing shifty about his manner, and nothing that I—having known him in childhood—found physically impossible to believe.

His basic aim his whole life had been to pursue happiness. And his chosen means to this, he happily confessed, had been to drink, smoke, get loaded, and get laid as often as possible. He'd run away from the good Christian home in his early teens by convincing a buddy to toss him into an open freight car. He was soon captured by the authorities and returned home, but he just kept finding accomplices and escaping via the same sack-of-potatoes method. He ended up riding the rails all over the West, became a justifiable legend in dozens of train yards and skid rows, but let the air out of the legend somewhat by answering to the absurd nickname "Shorty."

His first sexual experience had been with a prostitute, but he made it clear to me (though I made no comment) that this was a one-time deal. His sexual alliances now, he wanted me to know, were based on mutual attraction. He personally (he said with a jackhammer laugh) was attracted to *all* women, but to his ongoing amazement and gratitude a lot of women were also attracted to him. Being found desirable was clearly the surprise of his life. But I can't say that I was surprised. Predictability is, for many of us, the death of erotic feeling, and a first encounter with Eddie would certainly not be predictable. One could see at a glance how lithe and powerful his torso was. And condensed personalities exude a condensed form of attractiveness; as does courage; as does gratitude. There are advantages, as well, to a man who can't lift more than a finger to harm a woman. And so many men walk out. Eddie, at best, wobbled.

The low point of his life (and it had apparently come recently) was a stay in a mental institution. It was, he said, a trumped-up charge of attempted suicide that brought on the incarceration. He'd been staying in a Northwest Portland halfway house run by a staff that, he felt, hated him. The house had a ban on alcoholic beverages—an infringement on his openly professed philosophy of life. So when a friend snuck a half-gallon jug of red wine into Eddie's room, he pinched it by the neck between his own neck and shoulder, and tossed it up for a drink (I'd seen him do this, at age eight, with a half-gallon jug of apple cider). But the neck of this bottle broke, the falling glass cut his shoulder and a small vein in his throat, and when staff members ran in and found him in a sea of wine and blood, they accused him of trying to slash his throat and sent him to an asylum.

With the unpredictability I was coming to accept as his norm, Eddie told me he'd liked the asylum. It was simply the falsity of the suicide accusation that outraged him. He kept interrupting other stories all afternoon to express that outrage. He also interrupted other stories to express, to their faces, his admiration for passing coeds—and sure enough, he never saw one he didn't like. "I love my life," he'd growl after both kinds of interruption, as if challenging me, or anyone, to disagree. And I'd nod, open my tobacco tin, and feed his philosophy another smoke.

We went our ways after a while, our ways have never again coincided, and our childhood friendship and chance meeting bring me to no storybook conclusion. I had an almost-brother named Edward who has lived a life with just one finger. We've both traveled, one way or another, all over the West. We've both loved sex and hated liars. And the middle-aged face he wore in his twenties was no lie; if he's still living today, he has once again surprised me. But length of life, like length of body, was nothing Eddie chose to desire. My best hope for his life, like my best hope for my own, is that we remain able, to the end, to love it.

Writer **DAVID JAMES DUNCAN**, a lifelong Oregon resident, recently pulled up stakes and moved to western Montana. He's working on a third novel and a collection of stories, trying to follow the tremendous commercial success of his first two works of fiction, *The River Why* and *The Brothers K.*

◇

Duncan was born in Portland to a large family that included adopted siblings and foster children. "Both my mother and grandmother were devoutly religious, and both my grandfather and father weren't religious at all," he says. "But my grandmother was the family matriarch. She was the one who I, as a religious rebel, had to more or less defeat in 'dharma combat.' As a result I was disinherited. Yet I gained her respect. I held her hand while she died, and her last words to me—this was a couple of years ago—were, 'I love you, David.'"

Duncan began writing stories in the second grade. By junior high he was an "A" student and a three-sport athlete, "probably on the doctor or lawyer track," with equal abilities in literature and math.

"But when my brother died [of heart disease at the age of seventeen] I began to come unglued," he continues. "It took a while for me to realize it, but whatever religious faith I'd had was shattered. And my faith in the culture—the medical establishment, our family preachers, my schoolteachers—was also broken. Everything felt open to question. I moved from a completely closed view of the world to a completely open one. And it was terrifying for a while. But the terror began to abate when I found new brothers, not often with rote answers, but at least asking the same questions. And these brothers had names like Kerouac, Hesse, Mann, Suzuki, Melville, Thoreau, Kazantzakis, and Snyder.

"You know, this is an odd aside, but the facts of my life as a teenager can't be expressed without making me sound sexist, or at least utterly biased toward male writers. And in a sense it's true. Yet it's the *women* in my life who played the role of 'patriarchy.' The men in my life were mostly bewildered onlookers, while the women —especially my grandmother, but my mom, too—tried to force me to the patriarchal church, the elitist dogmas, the destructive industrial jobs, the corn-pone Cold War patriotism, and the materialistic world view that dominated our culture. My only allies in resisting the masculine attacks of these women were the writers—all men—who I just mentioned."

◇

Coming to terms with his brother's death while still in high school, Duncan began to pursue writing through correspondence with a friend at Stanford University. "This guy—his name was John, same as my late brother—would send me reading lists and books from his humanities classes, and his impressions of the books, and his own ideas about them, too. And I'd read them and do the same in return. And this was so much more exciting than anything going on in my classes that I basically became a satellite student of *his* curriculum. All this reading and letter writing was, by far, the best thing in my life at the time, and the most healing thing."

This required, however, Duncan's self-destruction as a high school student. "It was a suicide I gladly committed," he says, "but it was awful for my poor parents. First I quit church. Then I quit sports. Then I shit-canned my grades. I wanted to live in the counterculture, you see (I thought there was one, at the time). To make sure the devils of the Industrial World couldn't tempt me by recognizing that

I had some employable intelligence, I even got stoned before taking my SATs. So there were some bad blow-ups with my parents. But their marriage was failing at the same time. We were a busy family! So I basically became autonomous at seventeen, going where I wanted, doing what I wanted. And later—after they'd completely given up on me, and granted me freedom—my parents and I again became close."

Through the recommendation of a teacher friend, Duncan got into a program at Portland State University in which he "basically just read great books with men and women who were a lot smarter than me." He was hoping to become a writer. He studied English, Russian, American, and Asian literature, history, and a little philosophy, and kept up his correspondence with his Stanford friend. He kept a journal, in which he wrestled with ideas, "but it was mostly just dementia. What is expressible, and what isn't? Every writer needs a sense of this, and my journal taught me what isn't."

◇

Duncan earned his college degree in three years. He then spent two months in India—two months that, he says, changed his life. With no regard for his bachelor's degree and no desire to go to graduate school, he began to divide his time between writing and part-time jobs. He tended bar, mowed lawns, drove trucks. "Fiction is the only kind of writing I really wanted to do—the only kind that didn't remind me of homework assignments back in high school. So I preferred to indenture my body rather than my mind."

In the mid-seventies, he began working on "a very serious novel" about how Christmas had lost its meaning and become a mercantile thing, "the Great Christmas Exposé." But, he says with a grin, "these fishing

chapters kept popping out and they were wrecking the tone, because they were funny."

He eventually gave up on the Christmas story and began *The River Why,* a "serious comedy" about fishing and family and "the ultimate meaning of life. I was ambitious." For three years he juggled lawn-mowing jobs with writing. Then it took two years to find a publisher. "All the big publishers rejected it, so I was trying alternative presses and university presses when a poet friend, Sandra McPherson, told me to send it to Sierra Club Books." Sierra Club Books had no fiction program, but with Duncan's novel, they began one. After its initial publication, *The River Why* went to the Book-of-the-Month Club and to Bantam Books as a trade paperback. This success provided Duncan with enough financial support for a year and a half of solid writing. He began three novels and a collection of short stories simultaneously.

Duncan remarks that readers of his books always want to know if his stories are taken directly from life. "They want it to be your autobiography," he says. "But fiction is like a symphony score. The author is just the composer. And the book is inert, it's dead if some reader/conductor doesn't come along and perform it in the orchestra of their imagination. That readers are capable of this is awesome. And they are belittling their own awesome power when they want the story to have something to do with the actual, comparatively trivial facts of my life.

"The facts of my life are ninety percent irrelevant to my fiction. Facts can be boring little things that get in the way of truth. It's the way life makes us feel, it's universal human experience that fiction, the best fiction, deals with. I try to use these big feelings to compose a score I hope the reader will be able to perform. And when a reader does recreate one of my stories—including points of view they may violently disagree with—it's a hugely creative act on their part, and a gift to me."

Duncan maintains that his characters grow in ways he can't predict. "I had heard authors say that characters 'come to life,' but I never quite believed it till it happened to me. When you've written a synopsis, when you need Character X to be a certain type to make the plot work, and suddenly Character X becomes someone utterly different and your synopsis is useless and your plot shattered, that's when things have really started to work! In *The Brothers K*, this happened over and over. I didn't know Irwin would lose his mind, didn't know Papa would die, didn't know that some of the Adventists would become admirable in the end, didn't know my planned tragic ending would soften and become compassionate, or at least bittersweet."

With recognition of Duncan's work came concerns about stardom. "I never wanted to use writing to make myself larger or more visible," he says. "I don't want to be the star of my own stories. Of course I have to write of things I understand . . . But I enjoy anonymity. Maybe part of the reason for that is that I am one Caucasian male who wishes that most every-

thing that other Caucasian males have accomplished, planet-wide, for the past three centuries, could be undone. But it's also a spiritual proposition.

"Self-effacement makes writing more powerful, in my opinion, because it makes empathy possible, and empathy is what makes characters believable and compassion possible. So to heck with I, Me, My. When I/me/my am doing my/me work and it's going well, I don't know who I am, or where. A bumbling servant sits staring at the life showing itself in the story, trying not to interfere. That's how it feels. And it's a nice way to spend a workday."

◊

Duncan's move from Portland to Lolo, a small town outside Missoula, has meant a major change for him and his family. He and his wife, Adrian Arleo, a sculptor, have two young daughters, as well as a son from his first marriage. Duncan's study is in the house. He has insulated walls and installed a heavy door, and wears industrial earplugs to "keep things quiet."

After the "Reagan/Bush ransacking of the Cascades and the Coast Range," Duncan says, he lost his ability to love parts of Oregon. "I still dearly love much of the state, but I'm bitter about what happened to the part I loved best. Salmon and trees and indigenous animals have no voice except for the voices of the humans who love them. I tried to express that love in my writing. But my love was losing its object. Nature is a tapestry, and the Coast Range tapestry was, still is, in shreds. I don't know how to feel love for the ghost of a coho salmon, or the vast, choked Doug fir tracts of the corporate tree farms. So I've moved back in among things I *do* spontaneously love."

And Still the Subject Was Weather

Colleen J. McElroy

There is a story in my family about an aunt—my grandfather's sister, according to the story—who, in the late twenties, drove by herself from St. Louis to Chicago. For women in that era, going anywhere alone earned them the label "fast," but for a woman, especially a black woman, to travel alone through the Midwest in a spanking-new car during the time when women were supposed to stay home with their families, a time when black folks were segregated by law and income, was enough to earn my great-aunt the tag "fast and foolish." Forty years later, that was how my mother more or less described me when I told her I was moving to the West Coast.

"You better keep yourself to home," she said. "Always got to be doing something nobody else is doing. You better stay here with family and folks that can see for you. Don't know what all's out there."

But that was the point—I didn't know. And like my great-aunt, I had to see for myself, not wait for the family to "see for me." Of course, I understood that my mother's cautions were rooted in real fears for my safety. Reports of night riders, cross burnings, and lynchings had been as prevalent in her youth as crack houses, police brutality, and snipers are in today's news. And women, especially black women, were always vulnerable. But that was my second reason for wanting to leave the Midwest. I was a single mother with two children, and the encroaching blight of urban decay was a scant few blocks from the front door of the small ranch-style house where we lived in Kansas City. At night, I listened as sirens screaming along Swope Parkway joined those howling down Pershing Road until, by two or three o'clock in the morning, the dry culverts banking Brush Creek Boulevard were filled with one continuous cry, a sound I'm sure had not been heard since packs of wild coyotes had raced along those same creek beds.

Too often, I saw evidence of the night's activity during the day: from the swirls of debris dancing like dust devils on unswept streets, to the arrival of head-injury patients released from the county hospital at the rehabilitation unit where I worked as a speech pathologist. Not all of my clients were trauma victims who had been caught in the crossfire of the city's nightlife, but all were suffering from "neurological insult," as any damage to the brain and nervous system was called. In addition to those suffering from diseases, birth injuries, and strokes, I saw clients who had lost speech and language functions because of the insult of job-related accidents. Despite my need to be objective, those clients with farm injuries were as compelling to me as those who suffered the trauma of urban accidents, perhaps because so much of what happened in the city seemed to roll off the relentlessly flat countryside, where the air was as dry as old corn stalks and the rigidity of the landscape was reflected in the attitudes of the people.

The Midwest houses much of the Mason-Dixon Line, that nineteenth-century barrier between the slave states and abolitionist territory, a historical demarcation in the fight between slavery and freedom. Knowing the Midwest as I did, it was no wonder to me that the Supreme Court's landmark decision in *Brown v. Board of Education* was pulled from Kansas turf. That part of the country seemed to be subject to extremes in temperament and weather dominated by parchment-colored prairie that by size alone presented endless possibilities—all of them collared by the rashness of landscape and thermal conditions, all of this enough to make even the most reasonable inhabitants lose their sense of perspective. One shift in weather could send us reeling for cover or leave us irrationally accepting the difference as drastic but inevitable. Ask Dorothy.

So, one spring—after a winter of snowstorms that often blocked my front door with four-foot drifts, and a thaw that brought flash floods, tornadoes, and the promise of a summer so hot that humidity would exceed temperature—I set my son's world globe on the dining room table and gave it a spin. I'd planned to consider at least three choices, barring mid-ocean destinations and climates colder than Kansas'. On the first spin, my finger landed on Chicago. Dismissed—my great-aunt had already tried there. The second spin was mid-Atlantic. Dismissed. The next was Algeria. Not with two grade-school children in tow.

I was beginning to despair. Had the globe deserted me as well? Were those all the possibilities the world could offer? Even Dorothy had managed her escape to Oz on the strength of a pair of shoes. I tried again. Bingo! The British West Indies, somewhere between the Bahamas and Trinidad. There, I surely would have no problems with the weather. I decided to push my luck with one final spin. This time, my finger touched down on Washington State. Cold? The almanac said the Japan current and easterly winds produced temperate weather.

My mother said, "I don't know a soul who's ever been out there. And I don't care what's in that almanac, that's way north, up in the mountains. You're gonna be knee-deep in snow."

Mountains? I looked out my kitchen window toward the highway, to where a giant balloon advertising Big Boy Tire Center was the only thing breaking the evenness of the horizon. The next week, I sent an application to Western Washington State College in Bellingham to teach speech pathology. I had not envisioned myself as a teacher any more than I had envisioned living in mountainous country. But it would ease one of my mother's fears, that I would have no income; as she said to me, "Teaching is something you can always fall back on." (I'd certainly had no inclination to become a writer, either. With the exception of Phillis Wheatley and Paul Laurence Dunbar, all the poets and writers I had been introduced to in the classroom were male, white, and dead. Gwendolyn Brooks and Langston Hughes were introduced to me through black-history celebrations.) But the prospect of moving offered a life I was determined to see for myself.

I guess I didn't quite inherit all of my great-aunt's bravery. My trip across the country was not done solo. I helped my teenage brother get his driver's license, and on the 1,800-mile journey to the coast, I taught him the skills of driving under varied road conditions—although from time to time I imagined I was alone, sitting high in the front seat like my great-aunt in her 1920s Ford. Alone or not, it was an adventure with a payoff as big as the ocean.

After highways that stretched out flat as ribbons through Kansas, Nebraska, and half of Wyoming, we entered Montana and mountain country. From that point on, the world seemed made up entirely of mountains, regal hulks that glowered from a distance and then, to my Kansas eyes, threatened to send us careening off cliffs once we were on the necklaces of roads surrounding them. Even today, when I drive through the Olympic National Forest or the Cascades, I am reluctant to follow trucks that block my view of the road ahead for fear the road will end in midair, without warning.

But it was in those twists and turns of mountainous terrain that I succumbed. Not to the treachery of the highway, but to the sheer weight of wondrous landscape glistening in bright sunlight one moment and then, in the next, when we'd rounded a curve, brooding in dark green shadows. That was my first real sense of the Northwest coast: driving through dense green woods along a road that traced the rim of a bowl-shaped curve, then suddenly below us, a sweep of ocean rolling out in a great skirt of water laced in foam. It was love at first sight, a view that is still breathtaking three decades later. But on my first glimpse of the ocean, with a mountainside of evergreens rising away from it, I could only parrot Dorothy when she found herself in Oz.

"I don't think we're in Kansas anymore," I told my brother.

It took the better part of a year before I really could believe the Pacific Northwest was my home. That first autumn, when cold weather had already begun to claw its way across the Plains States, my children and I gathered wildflowers and stole honey from beehives along the slopes of Mount Baker, its snow-cone top incongruously set above the lush green of the lower slopes where we strolled dressed only in light sweaters. And in the winter, if I walked to campus early in the morning, I saw deer come down past the snow line to browse in the scrub brush on the hillside between my house and the college. In February, I held my son's seventh birthday party aboard the Lummi Island ferry. As we returned to the mainland—and as I counted and re-counted all those little boys, making sure I hadn't left one of them still running full tilt around the tanks at the fish farm—I watched mist roll in from the Strait of Juan de Fuca and head for the mountains. On any given day, I could start the morning near the ocean and end the day in the Cascade forests. Even Dorothy couldn't have changed directions that fast.

But I was still infected with midwestern skepticism and truly thought no amount of cinematic scenery could persuade me to trust the climate. Besides, always there was the rain. Then, in the spring, when my mother called during a snowstorm that had blanketed the midsection of the country from Nebraska to Illinois, I discovered how in only one winter I had begun to become acclimated to Northwest weather.

"I don't have to shovel the rain," I'd laughed when my mother asked how I was faring.

After her phone call, I'd opened my window to the rain and finished reading student papers while listening to its music. The air was sweet, so clean it could have been bottled. Years later, I would write a poem entitled "The Lover Romanced by Rain," but on that day I was aware only of how far away I was from Kansas weather.

Admittedly, I thought I had shed most of my Kansas life somewhere on the uphill climb, where the road slipped into evergreen forests and wound its way toward the ragged Northwest coast. I had moved to the Northwest during the years when hippies were in residence from California to Canada, and spring was marked by southbound brants and Canada geese flying above those northbound flower children northbound from California. It was the sixties and, as Bob Dylan crooned, the times they were "a-changin'." It was a time of sit-ins, be-ins, and showdowns. Those sparsely attended rallies I had joined in Kansas, rallies calling for voters' rights and equal education, had infected the entire country. And instead of listening to patients stumble through the maze of insulted neurological systems, systems that invariably failed them when they most needed language, I listened to political activists, street poets, and performance artists eloquently berate the American political system for its insult to the civil rights and personal liberties of black folks, of young men sent out to fight senseless wars, and of women denied the dignity of self-determination. Language did not fail them, and I was swept up in a mood of radical politics that I had never imagined in the presence of devil winds dancing across the prairie.

When I'd received my mother's "care" packages of flour and sugar in those first few months after my move to the Northwest, I'd sent back lists of all the grocery store chains, farmers markets, and interstates that made it unnecessary for me to mush through the snow by dogsled, which my mother was convinced I needed to do living so far north. But I hadn't told her about the incidents of racism that students protested on campus, or about the copies of still-active "sundown laws" quoted from the city courthouse records after an African diplomat's son was arrested for not having any "visible means of support." As scurrilous as these incidents were for Bellingham and the western Washington coast, they were not as abominable as the murderous racism in other parts of the country. It was true that in the Northwest, racism and intolerance usually took more subtle forms than the flagrant violence of the South or the ghettoized oppression of Eastern cities; but perhaps it was that shell of tolerance, in an age of intolerance, which allowed protests to move somewhat more quickly to discussion in this part of the country than in some other regions. Or perhaps it was that the entire country had been caught in the throes of political and social change, and we were stunned into action by the more outspoken heroes of the era, from Fannie Lou Hamer and Medgar Evers to Angela Davis and Malcolm X, who were revered, reviled, and, too often, assassinated. Whatever the reason, we did not have to count the number of shots that marked an execution before we understood the violence that had spread throughout the nation.

I had come to live in the Pacific Northwest between the assassinations of Jack Kennedy and Bobby Kennedy, of Medgar Evers and Martin Luther King, Jr. I had arrived at a time when the country, which claimed it prided itself on freedom of speech, faltered under a wave of assassinations and terrorism against those who dared to exercise that freedom. The irony of trying to train patients to regain language while I witnessed the swift and terrible condemnation of those who used language so persuasively was not lost on me. I could not give language back to voices silenced forever, but I could work toward empowering those who had yet to be heard. Not only was I teaching college classes in speech pathology, but I also began to work with government education programs, and hosted a television talk show that drew criticism for its open discussion of political views. (Within a year, a friend told me he thought my name had been added to an FBI list, and one morning my children reported that instead of the one man we'd seen watching our house for the past few days, now there were two men sitting on the front seat of the dun-colored Ford near our mailbox. Either lone surveillance was boring or I'd been moved to a higher priority; I never found out, because they both left two weeks later.)

At least twice a month, I flew to other parts of the country to evaluate education programs sponsored by the Office of Economic Opportunity. I left the diamond sparkle of Puget Sound waters and the mountains I'd come to love to make forays into what I considered the real world of conflict. And more than once, I returned to the coast while behind me an inner city exploded or a peaceful demonstration turned ugly with dogs and cattle prods. Each time I returned to the Northwest, I felt a rush of belonging as my plane banked over Puget Sound, the same rush I felt as I neared Bellingham along the familiar cut of road in the mountains near Lake Samish. But my hold on the area, as it was on any place in this country at that time, was tenuous at best. I seriously reconsidered moving to the British West Indies, my first "touchdown" point on the globe—except that I was hooked, by both the landscape and spirit, to my new home.

While initially I thought I had moved merely to escape the extremes of Midwest weather, now I was beginning to consider the pervasiveness of American racism, whether in the Northwest or any other part of the country. In the course of examining those issues, I eventually turned from speech pathology to a study of crosscultural perspectives on language. I still was not far away from a motto that I'd hung in my office in the speech pathology clinic at the college: *Language is a steed that carries you to a far country.* Except now, that far country was closer to home—a world described not just in terms of black people and white people but also Asian, Pacific, Spanish, Latin-American, and Native American. The center of my world was no longer the eye of a tornado or the tangle of a winter storm on the Mason-Dixon Line; now it extended from the Pacific Rim to South America, from the North Slope to Nogales. Instead of patients and doctors and rehabilitation specialists who, despite all of the "whole person" theories, invariably worked with symptoms, I was now in touch with poets, painters and sculptors, dancers, and actors, all of them invested in the sixties mood of brotherhood and world peace.

And my mother, who had predicted trouble when I moved to the coast, was convinced that trouble had arrived when I told her I was no longer pressing my hair but wore it natural, in an Afro. I barely gave her time to recover from that bit of news before telling her I was going to marry a poet.

"How'd you get mixed up with those kind of folks?" she asked.

How indeed? They seemed to be everywhere, like the mountains and crystal-clear bodies of water. In my neck of the woods, there were no enclaves of painters, poets, sculptors, and actors sequestered in some Greenwich Village or Soho away from an otherwise commercial populace. In the late sixties, my last years in Bellingham before I moved to Seattle and made a definite commitment to being a writer, I vacillated between teaching the intricacies of regaining language to students in speech pathology, and attending light shows and be-ins in face paint and outrageous costumes. I lectured on theories of language learning in between listening to protest poets who claimed, "*We* be the word sorcerers." I attended a *Dolce Vita* party for American and Canadian artists in an old brick factory in Sultan, Washington, and a reading of performance poetry to celebrate the opening of the Bellingham Museum in a baroque building that had once been the Whatcom County Courthouse. In the midst of all that, it wasn't much to move from admiring the artists I knew to becoming one.

My Afro hairdo was a look I had adopted, not simply because it was fashionable, but because it was incongruous to say I believed in change without demonstrating that I was capable of it myself. And while my attraction to poetry had begun with my love for a poet, I was soon caught up in the desire to do my own writing. Perhaps like my great-aunt wanting to take to the road alone, I wanted to see for myself just where poetry would take me.

Richard Hugo, the poet who had been my husband's mentor and friend, once told me that geography shapes the language of the poem. If so, the landscape of the Northwest presented some built-in dangers for me. But I began to write not out of the landscape but in spite of it. In the sixties, I heard a certain unconscious naiveté in the works of confessional and coffeehouse "hip" poets. When I listened to their poems, I realized that what little they knew about black folks had been drawn from stories of slavery and the media coverage of the latest riots, none of which connected with an impossibly beautiful landscape that seemed pulled off magazines like *Outdoor Adventure*. It was a landscape that reigned so majestically in the eyes of those poets that it provided insulation even against its own history: from the successful incorporation of the black township of Roslyn, Washington, or the knowledge that three out of five cowboys were black, to the ugly realities of the genocide of tribal cultures, and the detention camps for Japanese Americans during World War II. In my writing, I fight the urge to write with the gloss of scenic beauty, while acknowledging how much its very presence contributes to my voice.

This landscape often invades my poems—sometimes deflecting me, sometimes centering my work. In my collection of poems *Winters Without Snow*, written in the late seventies, when I was still grieving from a painful divorce, the landscape is prominent, acting as a "triggering town" (to quote Hugo's metaphor linking geography and poetry). While bemoaning the "gray smother of clouds" and "the constant drizzle," I also recall that out here, "the ocean is bigger than summer." But even under the dazzle of rain-forest mystique, I am wary. In "Haunting the Heart . . . " I caution my daughter to be aware of the lover, who is

> like an eagle
> miles above a dense forest
> haunting the heart
> he hears
> beating only for him.

And in a poem to celebrate my son's eighteenth birthday, I tell him to remember how "the ocean [is] roaring even when no one is listening." I have gone to the ocean just to listen to the heartbeat of the sea. It is a constant pulse that seems always to draw me to it—a bridge between where I am and what I remember—and like the weather, it can dominate my moods and, inexplicably, my memory. Although my front window allows me a view of the craggy silhouettes of the Cascades to the east and the Olympic chain in the west, the bulk of my writing still draws upon my life outside of the Pacific Northwest and my travels abroad. But when I am asked if my writing is dependent upon my living on the coast, I answer, Where did barn owls go before there were barns? I write from the perspective of where I am, and while I have often acquiesced to this geography, traces of the Midwest run like quicksilver through my work.

Yes, I am affected by the mountains, by the ocean and the many lakes, by the absence of snow and the presence of rain, but I also have learned how to use this landscape as a bridge between where I have been and where I need to go. It is a catalyst that helps me see for myself where poems will take me. Because here, where the "rain sings like a sleeping pill," I know that

> I am home and full of calendars and postcards of
> rough paper . . .
> My passport is stamped with triangles of countries
> as complicated as talk-stories. I turn the camera
> toward me, waiting for the right angle of sun,
> the climate that will get the picture right.

COLLEEN J. McELROY, poet, writer, and professor, lives at the north end of Seattle's Queen Anne Hill, in a home filled with paintings, drawings, figures, and puppets from Southeast Asia, South America, Africa, Japan. She has published eleven books of poetry and prose, including a textbook on language development.

◊

McElroy was born and raised in St. Louis. She attended two years of college in Europe after her father, a career army officer, was transferred to Germany. When the family returned to the United States, she attended junior college in St. Louis, then transferred to Kansas State University.

"I wanted to be an actress," she remembers, "but the only roles for black females were for maids. Instead, I took courses in radio and dance." She supported herself by teaching dance, especially Afro-Cuban and Latin, which brought her into contact with students from the Caribbean living in St. Louis and Kansas City. McElroy also worked part-time in a speech clinic, and eventually majored in speech pathology. She went on to graduate study in audiology at the University of Pittsburgh, and worked with hearing-impaired persons.

McElroy married and had two children before returning home to Kansas and finishing a graduate degree in speech pathology. Her work focused on patients with language and speech-comprehension difficulties.

◊

In time she found herself working too hard, taking her patients' problems too personally. In 1965, she decided to leave Kansas. McElroy had never really liked the Midwest, anyway. "The flatness got to me," she admits. "It was enervating. I needed to see water, a lot of water. I wanted the terrain to be challenging." A single mother with two small children, she found a job teaching speech pathology at Western Washington State College and moved to Bellingham.

She lived there six years. "I came to know artists," she says, "and became actively involved in cultural events. I had always taken art classes and thought I had odd ideas. But I did not feel strange there in Bellingham." McElroy became interested in poetry as well, and married a poet.

Soon enough, she wanted to write, too. She went to the library and selected some literary magazines to which to submit her work.

"I had twelve poems; I sent eight poems, and six were accepted. I thought, 'This is easy.' But I think I was doing pre-writing all my life. I had told stories when working with my patients. My first poems were like stories. In fact, I still favor the narrative voice, and this has shown up in my fiction and memoirs. Writing became an extension of what was in me already." The emphasis on language, of course, was at the heart of her speech pathology career. "Language became my musical instrument. I was tuning my ear to the differences in speech and language patterns."

◊

McElroy left Bellingham in 1972, feeling that without another degree she might

be working in a speech pathology clinic forever. She already had published one book on speech and language development and one book of poetry.

"While I was committed to being a writer, I needed the Ph.D. to get into the more flexible schedule teaching affords," she says. At the University of Washington in Seattle she completed her doctorate in ethnolinguistics and language arts, studying folklore and cultural patterns. Her dissertation was on dialect differentials—how the English language is a composite of dialects. "I think some of my work now grows out of that study of linguistic and cultural patterns," she says.

She began teaching in the English department, eventually being named full professor in 1983, the first African-American woman to reach that rank at the University of Washington.

◇

When McElroy moved to Bellingham, she knew she did not want her children to grow up in the racially tense urban areas of the Midwest. "Bellingham was more sequestered, a smaller town which gave them a different perspective on the world," she says. "In Seattle there was more tension between racial communities; it was much more tangible. It became more difficult for my children when we moved to the city." Her children still live in the Northwest; her son works on a fishing boat and her daughter is a preschool teacher.

McElroy continues to be concerned about race relations: "Racism is an open-door concentration camp where the guards and prisoners are crazy. Notions of racism are the barbed fences. I see it in many ways. The university students I see are not acculturated to deal with racial difference—it's a challenge. I don't think that at this end of the country we discuss the privilege of color. We don't have an inner city like New York; we have varied geography where you can find a niche to hide in. People come here to find sanctuary." The less overt forms of racism found here are not talked about, she feels. It remains difficult for her to figure out what to do about that as a teacher.

◇

"Travel in the world allows me to see how different Seattle is," McElroy says. "It helps me to see the direct racism and sexism in other places." She has traveled to many countries of Western and Eastern Europe, Africa, Asia, and South America. She recently spent three months in Madagascar, a nation that had been colonized only sixty-five years, a very short time compared with most African countries. "I was not so much interested in seeing the flora and fauna there; I was interested in the people, the folklore, the cultural implications of their language."

In studying the poetry and folk stories of Madagascar, she visited storytellers, who still take an active part in the culture and are important to the political history of the country. "In Western countries, the poet's place is usurped by TV and literature, whereas the oral tradition and ceremonies are still intact in Madagascar, drawing families, the dead and living, together." McElroy is working on a book of her photographs and the folk stories she recorded from Madagascar.

◇

In 1990, fellow poet Rita Dove suggested to McElroy that she apply for a Rockefeller Foundation residency at a retreat in Bellagio, Italy. Receiving the grant, she went there in the spring of 1991. It was then that she began writing her memoirs. With her first subject, her travel to South America in 1977, she began to look for a global perspective for her work.

"I realized I needed to warm up to this memoir writing so I could make it not for just me or one person sitting in front of me, but for a larger audience," she says. "In Bellagio, I met an East Indian writer. She read the first draft of some of my stories and said, 'What is this? You need to make it sing like your poems.' I knew then I had to drop the reportage voice. I needed to allow the voice to go where it wanted to go."

Since then, she has written on subjects such as traveling to a conference on African-American affairs held in Paris, and her struggle with foreign languages, as well as the usual encounters in marketplaces and villages. "The book is unusual because no one expects black people, especially women, to travel."

McElroy has used her writing to discuss social/political issues and how they affect her work and that of other black women writers. She says improving the recognition level for black writers is a hard-fought battle, but the situation is bound to improve for a number of reasons. "We are getting fragments of victory, but there are steps forward and backward; the Nobel Prize for Toni Morrison was a great step.

"Back in the sixties I thought I was the only black woman writer besides Gwendolyn Brooks," she says. "I didn't know about the many others; I had no black women poets

as teachers. I had no idea who to contact. I went to poetry readings and heard white poets trying to tell me who I am. But I had to do it myself." McElroy was stunned once when a colleague asked her if "there is enough black literature to teach a whole course." She says the notion persists that the writings of black people can be covered in the last week of an academic quarter—and even that often doesn't include the work of women.

McElroy points out how students of literature in other countries have studied and know American writers of color. In her piece "The Day I Was Alice Walker," she tells of an incident in the former Yugoslavia, where she attended a conference on women writers. As she sat with five African-American women scholars at a restaurant, the waiter said, "One of you wrote the Purple book."

"For his sake, one of us had to be Alice Walker, the writer of *The Color Purple*," McElroy says. "It was so important for us to recognize that we knew what he was talking about."

When she discovered that there was a community of African-American women writers, McElroy had to change her approach to writing. "I had to make parallels with others. I got to know the work of Sonia Sanchez and Lucille Clifton. I met others who knew my work—even Audre Lorde. That was the invitation into a community.

"At first they told me to get out of Seattle if I wanted to be well known," she says. "But if I lived in New York, I couldn't do what I'm doing. The frustration, the concerns would be very different. They say the West Coast is too laid-back; I say the East Coast is too uptight. Some New York writers adopt a particular kind of persona that deflects from their writing. Staying here, my writing has gone beyond one style of poetry."

Julia's City

Jonathan Raban

I came to live in Seattle in 1990, when I was forty-seven. It was late—very late—in the day for a new start. Literally so. At the departure gate at Heathrow Airport, it was announced that the flight would be delayed for an hour while engineers fixed a minor problem with the instruments. One hour grew, announcement by announcement, into ten, and it was dark when the plane eventually took off and we flew into the longest night I've ever known. There was a faint blue glimmer around the edge of the Arctic Circle, but otherwise the world was black. Working in the dim cone of light shed by the lens in the overhead console, my watch set to Pacific time, eight hours short of what felt like reality, I scribbled in a notebook through the in-flight movies and the meal services. I wrote excitedly about the life I hadn't yet begun to lead: I wrote about the companion whom (as it seems now) I barely knew; I wrote about the house we had not yet found to rent; I wrote about the book I hadn't yet written.

By the time the captain's voice came over the loudspeaker system to say that we were passing the lights of Edmonton, this unlived life was in perfect order on the page. There was the room, furnished with books, overlooking the water; the boat tied to the dock, within view of the window; the chapter steadily unfolding on the typewriter; my companion, pecking away at her computer within earshot. The scene was framed by fir trees, rimmed with sea. It included a softly lit restaurant, Italian, with the level in the bottle of Valpolicella sinking fast; the voices of friends, as yet unmet; the unbought car in which we scaled a logging track over the high Cascades; long sane days of reading and writing and talking; rain on the roof; a potbellied wood stove; love in the afternoons.

Looking back at the scribbler from a three-and-a-half-year distance, I see (of course) that he's a flying fool—a middle-aged man, inflated with unlikely hopes, trying to defy the force of life's ordinary gravity. Sailing over the wilds of Alberta at 38,000 feet, in time out of time, there's only one direction for him to move in and it's *down*. At best, he deserves to figure as the fall-guy hero of a comic novel.

Yet the West wasn't settled by realists. I think of James Gilchrist Swan, walking out of a deadly marriage in Boston in 1850, to take a ship for California and what would soon become the Washington Territory. In the same year, Dr. David Maynard walked out on his wife and family in Ohio, set off on the Oregon Trail for Puget Sound, and became a founding father of Seattle, the city's first real-estate magnate. Swan was thirty-three, Maynard forty-two, at a time when those ages were a good deal older than they are now. The graveyards of the Pacific Northwest are packed with people like Swan and Maynard—last-chancers, who left their failed businesses and failed marriages back East, hoping, against all experience to the contrary, that things might yet work out differently for them.

Jolting clumsily from cloud to cloud, its engines working in disquieting bursts and hiccups, the plane lost an awful lot of height in no time at all, and suddenly we were there, swaying low over Seattle. Lake Union was a black hole encircled by light; a late ferry, like a jack-o'-lantern, hung suspended in the dark space between Elliott Bay and Bainbridge Island. We scraped over the tops of the banking and insurance towers of downtown, and as the aircraft steadied itself on its glide path, I felt a rush of dizzy panic at what I'd done.

◆

We found a house on Queen Anne Hill and furnished it from yard sales, joining the Saturday-morning drift of cars with out-of-state plates and people with out-of-state accents. The idea that my own move was a strikingly bold and original one was blown clean away at the yard sales, where everyone in sight was hastily patching together the ingredients of a new life. We were all chasing the same old things, hoping that their comfortable and well-used air would rub off on us and make us feel less keenly our own awkward novelty in the landscape. I bought a couch on which, I speculated, the sixteen-year-old Mary McCarthy might have been found necking with the painter Kenneth Callahan in 1928, when the precocious McCarthy was making her debut in the White Russian bohemia on the south slope of Queen Anne. Saturday by Saturday, the house filled with congenial bits and pieces, each one somewhat scratched, or stained, or tarnished, or in need of glue or reupholstering; within six weeks it looked as if we might have been living in Seattle all our lives.

I was a newcomer in a city of newcomers, where the corner grocer came from Seoul, the landlord from Horta in the Azores, the woman at the supermarket checkout from Los Angeles, the neighbor from Kansas City, the mailman from South Dakota. Every so often I would meet someone close to my own age who was born in Seattle—but it nearly always turned out that their parents had moved here during the Boeing boom of the early 1940s. It is comfortingly hard to feel a misfit in a society where no one you know exactly fits; but to live, rootlessly, among so many other uprooted people does tend to make you feel like a guest at some large, well-appointed but impersonal hotel. Seattle manners seemed like hotel manners: civil, in the chilly fashion of strangers keeping other strangers at arm's length.

There was another city, seen in rare glimpses and at a distance. Down by the Ship Canal, along Ewing Street, in the atmospheric tangle of cranes, ships, sheds, and floating docks, I eavesdropped on an older

Seattle. The tug captains from Foss Maritime, boatbuilders, marine engineers, and sea-entrepreneurs had a language of their own. They talked in gruff laconic wisecracks and were masters of the sly obliquity that takes the indirect route to the heart of the matter. Unable to contribute, I was happy to offer myself up as a sacrificial stooge in return for being able to listen. The talk was knowing, intimate, affectionate, and malicious by turns—closely akin to the London gossip that I'd left behind me. These people remembered each others' parents and grandparents; they could speak allusively, confident of being understood; their city was an intricate closed circuit, built on a deep reservoir of shared memories and shared labor in the shipping and timber industries. To an outsider, it looked like a far happier city than the Seattle I saw most of— the Seattle of the lone Green Lake joggers, the transplants, the anxious liberals in REI outdoor gear and Volkswagen Cabriolets.

The society of the Ship Canal made me feel homesick and threw my own situation here into sharp relief. Lacking a usable past, we newcomers were like amputees. Without a shared past, we were short of humor, short of intimacy, short of allusions and cross-references—short of that essential common stock of experience that makes a society tick. It was no wonder that living in Seattle sometimes seemed like perpetual breakfast-time at some airport Sheraton.

◆

At the Seattle Public Library I was struck by the busy prominence of the genealogy section. I'd always thought that digging up one's ancestors was an eccentric hobby, and that people who went in for it—Mormons, rescuing their dead relations for Judgment Day; English snobs, claiming descent from the belted earls of Loamshire—were to be given a wide berth. But in Seattle, suddenly hungry for history, I saw the point of trying to patch through a connection between oneself and the articulate and meaningful past. This was a place where everyone felt in need of a family tree.

Having no ancestors of my own in the Pacific Northwest, I bought some at a Queen Anne yard sale. They came in a job lot in a Red Delicious Washington Apple box and cost me fifteen dollars. The early birds had been picking at the contents of the box, but there were still more than a hundred sepia photographs left, some going back to before the Civil War. The early birds had missed a little book of portrait miniatures, taken by a Philadelphia photographer, showing an extended family, including four men in Union army uniforms and a platoon of grim-visaged aunts in mobcaps and crepe. Some photographs came from Maine, some from Albert Lea and Austin in Minnesota; but the bulk of the collection had been taken by J. Foseide, Artistic Photographer, of Buckley, Washington, and Pautske, Artist, of Auburn.

The name McNish was written in pencil on the back of a picture of a waterside lumber mill, its employees posing stiffly in line in the foreground. Sorting through the heap on the floor of my study, I found the ghost, at least, of a story. There was a Buckley man, mustached and pomaded, in wing collar and white tie. Though his nose was on the large side and his eyes seemed a little shallow, he looked handsome and self-assured, like a successful door-to-door salesman. From Austin, Minnesota, came a plump girl of high school age, sweet and pudgy, first found garlanded with flowers in a tableau depicting the Three Graces. Soon the man and the girl were in the same picture. Here they were with a baby. And another. And another. The first of the amateur snapshots showed the couple on a rowboat outing, with a son of ten or thereabouts. The woman grew, photograph by photograph, from plump to stout. She put her hair up in a not-too-tidy bun and in the course of a decade or less she lost her meek smile and took on an expression of exhausted resignation. Meanwhile the man's mustache went gray; he began to wear steel-framed specs and an Odd Fellows pin; at sixty or so he sat behind a great desk piled with ledgers, his hair still exuberantly full, though nearly white now. Someone had scribbled "Uncle Alonso and Aunt Ottie" on the back of one of the husband-and-wife pictures, but there was little else in the way of clues.

I drove to Buckley, an engaging town, its 1890s Main Street still largely intact, and plodded up and down the rows of tombstones in the cemetery, hunting for names and dates. I called up Murray Morgan, the Edward Gibbon of Washington State. In the newspaper archive of the University of Washington I scrolled through the *Buckley Banner* on microfilm. Bit by bit, I came to know the family in the cardboard box—and to anyone without ancestors in western Washington, I commend Alonso and Ottie Bryant as the perfect proxy forebears.

Alonso had grown up in Machias, Maine, where he was born in 1855. His grandfather had fought in the War of Independence and was proud of having once caused a British sloop to founder on a sand spit by putting out the light in the Machiasport lighthouse and erecting a decoy light a few hundred yards south of the harbor. Alonso himself was a boy during the Civil War, and would later remember carrying letters to the post office for the wives and girlfriends of Union soldiers.

In the first half of the nineteenth century, Machias had been an important port in the timber trade, but as the loggers moved westwards, the towns on the Maine coast drifted into recession. When he left school, Alonso Bryant worked as a casual laborer in the construction industry, but the jobs were few and far between. He went west—finding well-paid and dangerous work building bridges for the Northern Pacific Railroad as it crossed the Rockies and followed the Columbia River to Portland, Oregon. I've seen those huge black timber trestles on which the trains creep over the gorges, and imagine Alonso, aloft, guiding a swinging beam into its slot in the cross-hatching.

By the time the railroad reached Portland, he'd saved enough to set himself up in business as a builder and contractor—though not for long, because he evidently saw that the people who were making most out of the construction industry were the suppliers and merchants, not the builders themselves. What he wanted was a rapidly building town and a hardware store. He found Buckley.

He arrived in 1892. He was thirty-seven, a big, tough man with a dandy's taste in tiepins and starched collars, the points of his mustache oiled and twisted, his glossy hair trimmed close around the sides of his head. He swaggers through his pictures, and looks as if he knows that he can still turn the heads of girls.

Buckley, on the White River, south of Auburn, had been incorporated in 1890—a brand-new mill town standing in the middle of a desolate acreage of logged stumps. It had a brick main street, a newspaper, an opera house; it had great expectations. Picket fences enclosed dozens of swanky wooden villas in every phase of construction. Buckley was prime hardware-store territory.

Four years after Bryant's arrival, in the early summer of 1896, William L. McNish brought his wife and daughter to Buckley from Austin, Minnesota. (They weren't the first McNishes in town; a laborer, W. S. McNish, was reported by the *Banner* to have lost his tool chest in a fire at the sash and door factory in 1892.) Ottie McNish—the garlanded Euphrosyne—was seventeen, and not the most likely match for the forty-one-year-old owner of Bryant's Hardware.

Between 1896 and their eventual marriage in 1903, I've followed Ottie and Alonso through the social columns of the *Banner*, where Alonso makes a big splash and Ottie a few shy appearances. By now, Alonso was a justice of the peace, active in the Republican Party, a bachelor bigwig in great demand. Ottie's claim to public attention was her singing voice. She joined the Presbyterian choir and graduated to singing solos, as when she took a leading part in the oratorio *Under the Palms* at the Presbyterian church.

I see Ottie in the hardware store, dithering in the fastenings section, and Alonso, self-important, avuncular, thumbs in his buttonholes, setting her to rights. He smells of patchouli oil and cigars. (I know about the cigars because I now keep my business cards in a scuffed black-leather wallet, made for the purpose, that once belonged to him. It is lettered in gold-leaf: "Compliments of Julius Ellinger & Co. Havana Cigar M'frs Tampa Fla. and New York.")

For a muddy frontier town—and perhaps *because* it was a muddy frontier town—Buckley had an intense social calendar. Newcomers were immediately enrolled by the clubs, church groups, and Masonic lodges. In winter there were several musical evenings in private houses. Both Ottie and Alonso attended one at the home of Mr. and Mrs. J. F. Jones, where Miss Elisabeth Jones "rendered several choice selections in rich contralto." There were organized trips to Tacoma for Christmas shopping and to see the Ringling Bros. Circus. The town turned out for a demonstration of mental telepathy at the Opera House by Keller the Hypnotist. At the Women's Club, the mayor's wife, Mrs. McNeely, read a paper on Sappho and Mrs. Browning. The Buckley Dramatic Club mounted regular entertainments, including one of which I have a photograph (Alonso appears in it, resplendent in eighteenth-century wig and stockings).

In September 1903, the Bryant-McNish wedding merited seven paragraphs in the *Banner*:

WEDDING BELLS

At the residence of Mr. and Mrs. Wm. L. McNish, in Buckley, on Saturday, Sept. 19, at 7 o'clock PM occurred the wedding of their daughter, Miss Ottie R. McNish, to our well-known townsman, Mr. Alonso M. Bryant.

The wedding was a quiet one, only the near relatives of the bride and the wife of the officiating minister, Rev. O. E. Cornwell, witnessing the ceremony

After a delicious wedding supper the bride and groom departed on the evening train for a brief bridal tour to Victoria, B.C., and other points down the Sound.

A goodly number of friends gathered about them at the station, with congratulations and showers of rice. Their friends who are many wish them a very happy journey together through life.

They will soon be at home to their friends at their new residence on East Main Street, Buckley.

The bride is a young woman of reserved habits and is held in high esteem by all who know her. She has been a resident of Buckley for a number of years and her friends are not a few.

The groom is one of our hardware merchants and has been here for a period of eight or nine years. In that time he has built up a good business and is highly respected by all who know him. THE BANNER joins the host of friends in wishing them many years of unalloyed pleasure.

Ottie was twenty-five, Alonso forty-eight. Though in the pictures of the couple one might mistake Ottie for the older of the two, she is so ample and matronly, Alonso so spruce (I suspect him of dyeing his hair—or, possibly, of persuading J. Foseide, Artistic Photographer, to work some darkroom magic on it).

Ottie had babies—three sons and a daughter. Alonso went into local politics. He was on the school board and the town council. He was town treasurer and later mayor of Buckley. In 1913 he was elected to serve as a state congressman at Olympia. In the young and fluid society of western Washington, this rolling stone from the East Coast had become a fixed pillar of the community. In the portrait that I've propped beside the typewriter he is looking up from his papers in the state house at Olympia: his eyes swim behind his glasses; his broad mouth is set in a down-turned arc; he exudes that air of somber rectitude that might gain him election to high fiscal office. He looks too refined for his large practical hands, which he keeps closed, as if they embarrass him.

Ottie's health broke in her fifties and she died in 1935, aged fifty-eight, but Alonso continued to run the hardware store in Buckley, which spawned an offshoot, Bryant Hardware in Kirkland, managed by Alonso and Ottie's son, Mariner Bryant. When the United States entered World War II after Pearl Harbor, Alonso—who could remember his grandfather talking about the War of Independence, and who had himself lived through the Civil War—was still in business. He was eighty-seven, going on eighty-eight, in 1942, when he died at his daughter's home in Seattle on July 19. I was then five weeks old—old enough, by a whisker, to count this pioneer of the Pacific Northwest as living in my own lifetime.

◆

The newcomer here should at least be able to feel that he or she is in the historical swim of things, for the history of the Pacific Northwest since 1792 has been a history of newcoming and newcomers, a braid of interwoven Alonso-and-Ottie stories. The stories are all around us—in the fabric of the houses we live in, in the names of places and streets; they go begging at yard sales and can be fished out of dumpsters.

My own house (built in 1906 in the wake of the Alaskan gold rush, a creaky timber warren of rooms with sloping floors and doorways that have twisted out of true—a relic of another wave of newcomers to the region) stands just below Mount Pleasant Cemetery on Queen Anne Hill. I like to walk among the tombstones there, where so many of the dead are buried thousands of miles from where they were born. CARL EWALD, BORN NEAR MARIENWERDER, PRUSSIA, JUNE 12, 1817, DIED AT SEATTLE, WASHINGTON . . . ISABELLA BLAIR ORMSTON, NATIVE OF EAST LOTHIAN, HADDINGTONSHIRE, SCOTLAND . . . WILLIAM DICKSON, NATIVE OF BELFAST, IRELAND . . . ANNA LLOYD TINKHAM BORN MAY 28TH, 1849, WALES, ENGLAND [sic], DIED FEB 9, 1908, SEATTLE, WASH. One inscription pleases me particularly: SYLVESTER S. BOWER, BORN NEWFIELD, N.Y., APRIL 1854, CAME TO WASH. 1889, DIED JULY 12, 1936. That the date of his arrival in the Pacific Northwest should be commemorated as one of the three salient facts of Mr. Bower's life seems exactly right. That's how it feels to me, and how I want it on my own tombstone, please: . . . CAME TO WASH. 1990 . . .

You can't look out of the window here without seeing that you are in an uprooted and homesick land. Seattle's domestic architecture pines for a world elsewhere. The old German Club on Ninth Avenue, with its tall and narrow second floor windows, harks back to some tree-planted *Strasse* in nineteenth-century Hamburg or Cologne; the well-to-do English who settled around St. Mark's Cathedral on Capitol Hill had their own mullioned and half-timbered enclave of replica manor houses, their details copied from Chamberlain's *Tudor Homes of England*, the great architectural sourcebook of American mock-Tudor. Close by the English quarter, a graystone Russian *dacha* glooms over a lordly view of Interstate 5 and Lake Union. Down in the International District, the glum brick buildings with balconied shrines set high over the street are homesick for Shanghai, while the "classical" terra-cotta friezes of downtown, with their gargoyles and cartouches and anthemions, are homesick for history itself—anybody's history, and the older and grander the better. Stand near the corner of Third Avenue and Madison Street, and look up at the wild and dizzy conflation of Ancient Greek, Ancient Roman, English Gothic, Art Deco Egyptian, French Empire, Italian Renaissance, all handsomely molded in Green River mud. Out in the countryside, there are a Bavarian mountain town, a Norwegian fishing village, and, in the Skagit Valley to the west of Mount Vernon, an entire landscape that even a Dutchman (with a slight case of astigmatism) might plausibly mistake for the flat farms and poplar-fringed villages of Friesland.

What is true of the architecture and the landscape is even truer of people's domestic interiors here. When I first visited Seattle, to research a chapter of a book, I got used to the oddity of parking my car outside a ranch-style bungalow in a street of more or less identical ranch-style bungalows, then, inside the door, taking off my shoes and entering the cross-legged-on-the-floor life of the immigrant Korean family, with its rugs and carved chests. Outside lay Greenwood, or Ballard, or Phinney Ridge; inside, we were halfway back, at least, to Seoul or Inchon. When I came to live here, I found that half the houses I visited in Seattle were like this—nostalgic reconstructions of another time, another place. A ground-floor apartment turned out to be a Greenwich Village loft, the plaster on the walls hacked off to expose bare brick, the ceiling strung with decorative, non-functional plumbing. I'm writing this with a mild hangover, incurred at a party last night in the Madrona neighborhood; the American owners of the house were Anglophile enthusiasts of Early Music, and as one stepped through their front door one entered a sort of legendary Merrie England of shawms and sackbuts and psalteries, of

Morrismen and maypoles. The pictures on their walls were watercolors of the great Elizabethan piles, like Moreton and Hardwick halls; the books on their shelves had the sort of bindings that you rarely see outside the set on which Alistair Cooke used to introduce "Masterpiece Theatre"; the books themselves were described to me by an awed friend who had checked out the library in the downstairs bathroom as "works of medieval feminism." I like to think that the next-door neighbors were passionate Arabists whose living room was a faithful reconstruction of a merchant's *diwan* in a house deep in the Aleppo souk; or maybe tribal-Africa buffs, with a house full of spears, blankets, and goatskin drums.

For Seattle tends to slop about in time and space. In New York, you're rarely in doubt that this is New York and the time is the present, but there's less here and now in Seattle than in any city I've ever known. Its woody plots and inward-looking houses, screened from their neighbors by thick tangles of greenery, allow people to live in private bubble-worlds of their own construction. My neighbor's Seattle isn't mine—or yours. There are days when the city seems to me to be dangerously like an old-fashioned lunatic asylum: here's the lady who believes herself to be Anastasia Romanov; and here's Napoleon; and this gentleman is Alexander the Great; and here's a teapot . . . Seattle does not insist—as both bigger cities and smaller towns do—on its own overbearing reality: it is unusually indulgent to those of its citizens who prefer to live in dreams and memories. If you want to bury yourself in a cottage in the trees, pretending that you are living inside a nineteenth-century French novel, or that you're back home in another decade and another country, Seattle will do astonishingly little to disturb your illusion.

◆

My Seattle is a city of émigrés and migrants, and inevitably I see deracination as part of the basic fabric of the place. But I've planted a much deeper root here. My companion of the first paragraph of this piece became my wife, and we have a child, now a year old. My American daughter—a Washington Native, as they say on the bumper stickers.

Even now, I see our two cities diverging.

For Julia, the word "tree" already means the shaggy cypress and the drooping fir, whose inky green will never convey to her the alien and depressive associations that they have for me. To my English eye, the Douglas fir has a sort of grim splendor, but it seems to me a congenitally unhappy vegetable. To Julia's Pacific Northwestern eye, it's the most homely tree she knows; it's where the squirrels live and where the little pine siskins fuss and flutter.

So, too, the word "water" is coming to mean the deep and dusty stuff of Puget Sound, on which she has already been afloat. To me this water, which drops to more than a hundred fathoms just a few yards out from the shore, is uncannily, shiveringly deep, and queer things live in its ice-cold profundity, like *Architeuthis*, the giant squid, and the brainy, jet-propelled *Octopus dofleini*. I grew up in a country where wild things were rabbits and foxes; she is coming into possession of a world where killer whales live in the watery suburbs of her native city, where real bears raid trash cans on the outskirts of Everett and mountain lions are sometimes spotted in Gig Harbor. God knows what she'll make of the wild exciting world of Beatrix Potter's Lake District animals—Peter Rabbit and Jeremy Fisher.

Growing up in the mock-antique, mock-heroic architecture of Seattle, Julia won't be amused by its comedy or touched by its pathos, as I am; it'll just be old to her—as real Tudor and Jacobean architecture is old to me—and dull, in the way that merely old things are. When she gets to see Florence, and tires of the long hot hike around the Uffizi and Bargello, she may be fleetingly reminded of Seattle; as when she visits her English grandparents in Leicestershire, she may notice some battered, down-at-heel versions of buildings that are in a fine state of upkeep back home.

As children of migrants to the West must do, she'll grow up with a sense of distances unlike anything that either her New Yorker mother or I knew as children. Her maternal grandfather lives on the Upper West Side of Manhattan, her English grandparents in Market Harborough, and Julia has been born into a house where the phrases "back East" and "in England" are constant, almost daily reference points—where two shadowy worlds-elsewhere hover in the middle distance behind the world she lives in.

That is such a standard feature of West Coast life that I bet Julia will share it with half the children at her school. I've heard people born in this region talk of it as "out here," as if to be a westerner was to be in some sense, however faint and ancestral, in exile from the warm center of the world. I hope my daughter doesn't grow up to speak of her birthplace as "out here," and doubt that she will; if the present tilt of the world economy continues, if there's even a grain of truth in all the boosterish talk about the Pacific Century, then Seattle will be, and perhaps already is, a good deal closer to the center of things than are New York and London.

This is her city in a way that it can never be mine; and as newcomers must take their cues from the natives, I now have to learn about Seattle from Julia. I'm making a beginning. I'm relearning the meaning of the word "tree," and a whole enormous syllabus looms ahead. But I am—in my daughter's American English—a quick study. I'll get to figure it out.

JONATHAN RABAN is a recent transplant to Seattle from England, where he began his distinguished writing career. He first came to Seattle in 1989 to research a chapter for his book *Hunting Mister Heartbreak*. The visit was meant to last a month or six weeks.

◊

Raban was born in 1942 in a village in North Norfolk, a place as remote, he asserts, as a town on the Olympic Peninsula might have been at that same time. His father, a British artillery major, was absent during Raban's early years. After World War II, Raban's father entered a theological college and became a Church of England priest, and after that, the family moved every couple of years: to the outskirts of Liverpool, to Chichester in Sussex, Winchester in Hampshire, and Lymington in the New Forest.

Jonathan, the eldest of four children, entered boarding school at Worcester at the age of eleven, and stayed there until he was sixteen. It was a hateful experience. "I was miserable and inattentive, " he recalls. "I lived in a dream world."

He went on to the University of Hull, a place he calls distinguished in only one respect—that the librarian was the poet Philip Larkin. Still, his university years were "three years of heaven, immersed in books." Raban

had been writing since childhood and always saw himself as a writer. At seventeen, he had his first short story published in a national magazine, but, he admits, it was a flash in the pan. At the university he wrote "pretentious stuff and collected an impressive pile of rejection slips for my bad poems and stories."

Upon graduation at twenty-one, Raban went into the theater, getting a job as a bit-part actor with the Salisbury Repertory Co., on the strength of his theatrical experience as a student. "But I was no good at movement and was too tall," he says. "If I had continued on the stage, I would probably have had a career playing second policemen."

He quit after two months and sold brushes door-to-door for a while before returning to work on a graduate degree at Hull. His unfinished doctoral thesis carried the title "The Theme of Immigration in the Jewish-American Novel, 1874 to the Present."

"I can't remember quite how or why, but I got deeply interested in Jewish-American fiction while I was a student. I'm not a Jew, but it seemed to me that those Jewish heroes—in the novels of Henry Roth, Saul Bellow, Bernard Malamud—spoke to me in a way that the heroes of modern English fiction did not. Maybe it was the anxious rootlessness, their air of being strangers in the world, that caught my imagination. Whatever it was, they seemed to me to embody an important part of my own somewhat rootless experience."

Raban got a job teaching at the University College of Wales in the 1960s, "when higher education was a growth industry," and started to write books. His book *The Technique of Modern Fiction* grew out of the classes he was teaching with first-year students. "As a twenty-two- or

twenty-three-year-old, I loved teaching—life was an intellectual party for the eighteen months I was there," he remembers. "Then I got a better job at a smarter and brighter new university, the University of East Anglia."

As a lecturer in the school of English and American studies, Raban had the freedom to develop new courses rather than follow an old syllabus. But with the freedom came time-consuming responsibilities, among them chairmanship of the admissions committee. "Besides teaching and committees, I was trying to write academically, general criticism and reviews, and publishing short stories," he says. "I wrote a TV play and sent it to the BBC. It didn't get produced but I got another commission for a play for £900, an amount equal to half of my salary for a year's teaching. I realized then that I could support myself by writing—and that commission was a liberation."

◊

Raban went to London in 1969, at the age of twenty-seven, with a pocketful of commissions. He wrote in various genres: plays for TV and radio, short stories for *London Magazine*, book reviews for *The New Statesman* and later for *The Sunday Times*.

In 1973 he wrote his first book, *Soft City*, "an oddity, part fiction, part literary criticism, part autobiography and sociology—a story about the urban environment," he says. "I was passionate about interdisciplinary studies and impatient with narrow categorizations—*Soft City* says damn the genres."

"I think that there is a single long continuum which takes in all writing. One end of the continuum takes in myth and legend, but the other end is statistical reporting like scores in football or the location of a traffic accident. Let's say that the flat facts sit at the right side of the continuum

and the purest invention sits at the left side. Most writing of a generally imaginative kind falls somewhere near the middle. My works of 'fiction' actually belong somewhere to the right of things, while my works of 'nonfiction' belong more to the left. In other words, they may be, and not always for the best, more 'inventive' than a lot of novels.

"I like to think of all my own books, the 'nonfiction' and the 'fiction,' as sitting somewhere in the middle of the continuum. There's some imagination in all of them and there is a good deal of 'fact' in all of them, too. But I hate that hard generic line that says 'fiction' is creative and 'nonfiction' is merely reporting. That's hooey."

Raban's comprehensive approach to writing is evident in a group of foreign travel books that he began to write in 1977 when he took a magazine assignment to follow Dame Freya Stark down the Euphrates River in Syria on a raft. "Going to Syria was the first time that I really stepped out of my own culture."

Later, he took a synopsis of what would become *Arabia Through the Looking Glass* to a publisher, and received money to fund three months in the Middle East. "I took lessons in basic Arabic, then went to Bahrain, Qatar, Abu Dhabi, Dubai, Egypt, and Jordan. Then I wrote the book in eight months, a very fast book."

◊

Raban first came to the United States in 1972 to teach at Smith College, spent three months in the Boston/ Cambridge area in 1973, and then began to travel back and forth between Boston, London, and New York.

In 1979 he went down the Mississippi River in a sixteen-foot aluminum skiff with an outboard motor; the result was his celebrated book *Old Glory*. "I started from Minneapolis and headed for the Gulf of Mexico. The idea was to visit little towns and be part of the landscape, to learn about the river on a daily basis. I left on Labor Day and reached the Gulf on New Year's Day. There were some scares, a good deal of high social comedy, and some long stretches of miserable solitude."

By the time he got back to England from New Orleans, Raban had decided he hated small boats. But three weeks later he was still dreaming of the river. For a while he thought these recurrent dreams arose from a fear and dislike of being afloat. It took some time for him to realize that, on the contrary, they heralded a new addiction. They could be stopped only by buying another boat. "I got a sixteen-foot motorboat and kept it on the Thames, going up and down the river while writing *Old Glory* for two years, full time."

After finishing *Old Glory*, Raban took up a new project: to write about his homeland as if it were a foreign country. He bought a larger boat. "What I wanted to do was to sail round England, returning to all the places where I'd lived, but with the skeptical, stranger's eye of a visiting mariner from abroad.

"The whole thing was foolish—the only sensible thing I did was to hire a retired naval commander for three weeks of training. Then I set out to circumnavigate the British Isles, going counterclockwise, and spent four months afloat."

When he came to write the book, he found himself in trouble.

"I worked on it, on and off, for fifteen months. I had fifty unfinished pages and I hated them. The problem was that I was making myself out to be more alienated from England than I really was. To tell this story, I needed a character who really was a stranger to modern England. So I recast it as a novel. *Foreign Land* is about a sixty-year-old Englishman, George Grey, who has been out of England, working in the Middle East and Africa, for forty years. Writing his story, I found the words coming easily, and that novel is the book of mine, really the only book of mine, that I go back to with pleasure.

"When the novel was finished, I suddenly found it easy to write the book that had given me so much trouble three years before. *Coasting*, which came out in 1986, is my first-person, though I hesitate to call it 'nonfictional,' account of that trip around the British Isles."

For all his extensive travel and the chronicles he's written, Raban asserts that a writer's place is in his or her language. He puts it like this: "Language is where you live, it's a real place, more important than geography."

One Little Indian Boy

Sherman Alexie

I.

I am American Indian, Native American, Aboriginal, Indigenous, and All of the Above. No. I am Spokane/Coeur d'Alene. No. I am five-sixteenths Spokane and one-half Coeur d'Alene because my mother is five-eighths Spokane and my father is full-blood Coeur d'Alene.

My whole life has been about fractions.

I was born hydrocephalic in Sacred Heart Hospital in Spokane, Washington, on October 7, 1966. I was born with a skull that expanded on an hourly basis and underwent brain surgery before I was six months old.

The doctors told my parents I probably wouldn't survive the surgery. The doctors told my parents I would most likely be severely mentally retarded if I did survive the surgery.

My father had a Catholic priest baptize me and give me last rites. My mother snuck a Protestant minister in later to say a final prayer for me.

I lived. I learned to read just before my third birthday. I learned to read while I still wore diapers.

Still, the hydrocephalus changed everything. It changed the arrangement of my teeth and the construction of my backbone. It changed the shape of my eyes and the content of my dreams.

I had epileptic seizures until I was seven years old. I wet the bed until I was twelve.

I was a reservation television Movie of the Week.

The hydrocephalus changed everything. I read all the literature now and wonder if I was and am a Fetal Alcohol Baby. My mother and father were active alcoholics during my conception and gestation. My mother is a drug and alcohol abuse counselor now. She's been sober for twenty years, but I wonder if she cries when she reads about the prenatal effects of alcohol.

Still, I really did learn to read before I was three years old. I learned to read from a Superman comic book that my father bought for ten cents in Dutch's Pawn Shop in downtown Spokane. I remember that I cried for days after I lost the comic book. I still get weepy when I think about it.

I still get weepy when I drive down Main Avenue in Spokane, right past where Dutch's Pawn Shop used to be. Dutch's was torn down and the whole lot was paved over years ago. There's just a parking lot now in the space where part of my heart used to live.

There are parking lots in many places where parts of my heart used to live.

Is that overtly romantic and sentimental? Yes.

But I can tell you this. I don't ever park in that lot where Dutch's Pawn Shop used to be.

II

Why do I write? I get asked that question all the time, in various forms and for various functions. I suppose I can answer it best by answering it like a politician would—with another question:

"Sherman, why do you write?" the interviewer asks.

"Why wouldn't I write?" I answer.

I've never had to invent a stance as a writer. I've never had to pretend to be a western writer or a southern writer or a New York City writer. I've heard the Blackfoot writer James Welch say that Indian writers don't have to invent a stance, they already have one.

I live and write in Spokane, only twelve blocks away from Spokane Falls, that place where my tribes have gathered for thousands of years. Let me say that again. *I live and write in Spokane, only twelve blocks away from Spokane Falls, that place where my tribes have gathered for thousands of years.*

My ancestors, my grandmothers and grandfathers, fished for salmon on those falls before Jesus Christ ever walked across water. In fact, my grandmother Etta Adams told me that the salmon used to swim so thick in the Spokane River that an Indian could walk across the water on their backs.

"You don't think Jesus was walking on just faith?" she asked me.

My grandmother was a storyteller. My mother is a storyteller. Indians are storytellers. All deeply spiritual people are, by necessity, storytellers. The Bible is just a book of stories. The Koran is just a book of stories. But they are also more than books of stories. And in the same way, Indian stories are more than just stories. They are an exact reflection of a people.

Basically, I was born a storyteller. Every rock, in this little part of the West that is my home, has a story I know. Late at night, while I try to sleep in this city, I hear my river flowing just a mile away. No. I hear *our* river flowing just a mile away.

Don't you see? I don't have to defend or justify my position as a western writer. I don't need to be a western writer. I'm writing stories for and about people that were "here" many generations before "here" was called the West.

Besides, for non-Indians, whether they are writers or not, something else is always west of "here."

III.

I know about hate.

When I was eight years old, I waited with my family at a bus stop in Spokane. Dad had just received some money from his crops and had taken the whole family to spend the night in the big town. I remember those good times. Dad had money in his pocket. He had money.

We always stayed in the Park Lane Motel out on Sprague Avenue, right next to Kmart, just a mile away from the Trent Avenue Drive-In. The ceremony was always the same. We'd all pile into one room—my parents, big brother, and twin sisters—and eat hero sandwiches from the Kmart deli. Then, we'd all go down to the bus stop and head downtown for a while. I don't know why we always rode the bus downtown. We had a car. I guess it was the novelty of riding on a bus. We'd shop downtown and Dad would buy all of the kids a new T-shirt.

On one particular day, Dad bought me a Bruce Lee shirt and I practiced karate kicks all day long. Then, on that particular day, as we waited at the bus stop to head back to the motel, a white man walked by us. He stared at us with a kind of hatred I had never seen before. I have seen it since, often. But that was the first time I had ever seen that much hatred from anyone or anything.

"Fucking Indians," he said and spat at us.

No. He spat on us.

IV.

Every Indian is born political. When every aspect of our lives is governed by some bureaucracy or another, then it's impossible to avoid politics. Still, I do my best to avoid them.

I don't vote. Well, I didn't vote until the 1992 presidential election. I signed up and voted for Bill Clinton. It's not that I thought he was some kind of savior. I just wanted to make a stand.

But as I watch his presidency stagger under the weight of bipartisan animosity, I have come to realize that our lives can never be changed by any political action. That's to say, our lives cannot be changed by working within any established political system.

I don't trust this government at any level. All the politicians look like they could be low-level management types in the Bureau of Indian Affairs. My wife, Diane, who is Hidatsa, Winnebago, and Potawatomie, has a button hanging from the rearview mirror in her car that reads, SURE YOU CAN TRUST THE GOVERNMENT. JUST ASK AN INDIAN OR A WHALE. But my position as a cynical writer certainly isn't new. I don't have to be an Indian writer to be a cynical writer.

But as a cynical writer, as a cynical Indian writer, I find that my work is nearly universally qualified as "political" writing. It's placed in sort of a sub-genre. Actually, since Native American writing is itself a sub-genre, then Native American political writing would have to be a sub-sub-genre.

So, as a sub-sub-genre writer who has actually become critically and commercially successful, I am subject to some stupid questions.

I've been asked if my parents are literate, too. I've been asked why I don't write about "more" than Native Americans. I've been told how my work is influenced by writers I've never heard of, let alone read. I've been told that my work is existential, depressing, and filled with suicidal self-loathing.

No.

I write with love, with love for myself, for my tribes, for all Native Americans in general, and for very specific Natives.

I write about love.

I write about those moments so filled with love that I can barely stand it.

I write about the time my sister told me she could recognize me by the smell of my clothes.

"Junior," she said. "You could put a blindfold on me, line up a hundred guys, let me smell all of their shirts, and I could pick you out easy."

You see, I knew she meant to say "I love you," and I wrote it down. I wrote it down because it's true. The Acoma writer Simon J. Ortiz said that if it's fiction, it had better be true. Quite frankly, I've never had to make up anything. I don't know how much of an imagination I really have yet, because I haven't run out of stories that have actually happened.

A friend told me once that the characters in my books may be alcoholic, poor, and hungry, but at least they have each other, they have love.

Yes, we do. We have love.

v.

When I was little, living on the Spokane Indian Reservation, I used to love to hide. Well, I didn't always love it. Sometimes I had to hide because there were so many Indian boys who picked on me. I was beaten on a daily basis throughout most of my Indian school days.

I remember that Michael Sherwood, who has since died in a car wreck, sat on my chest and spat into my mouth for an hour. Michael wasn't some racist white guy. He was a Spokane Indian, one of my fellow tribal members. It's strange to remember how cannibalistic some of those Indian boys were.

Yes, I would hide in this cave. Actually, I took Diane back to that place where I used to hide, so she could see another part of my life. In my memory, that cave was huge. But it is actually a narrow space between rocks, not really a cave at all. I was disappointed.

Yet, I suppose memory always works that way.

When I used to drink, I would have these alcoholic dreams and remember them later as real. I once dreamed that I was there when Michael Sherwood was killed in that car wreck. I dreamed that I pulled him out of the car wreck while he was still alive. Barely alive.

"Help me," he said, blood flowing from his mouth.

I dreamed I sat on his chest and gave him CPR. I pressed against his chest, against his heart, and pumped blood out of him. Michael Sherwood tried to talk but the blood filled his mouth. He couldn't call me names anymore. He couldn't talk.

I dreamed all of that during an alcoholic stupor and was convinced it had happened. I apologized to everyone for my cruelty, for my ability to murder somebody. Then I would justify my behavior. He was going to die anyway, right? I just helped him along, eased his pain and suffering.

I used to get so drunk that I couldn't tell the difference between my dreams and my reality. I dreamed I went to Michael Sherwood's house on the reservation to tell his parents what I had done. I knocked and knocked on the door but nobody answered. When I woke up in the morning my knuckles were bloody. Which door had I been knocking on?

It seems like my memory, my whole life, has been overwhelmed with metaphor.

All day long, I say, "That would be a good poem." All day long, I say, "That would be a good story." Every aspect of my life takes on literary meaning. I'm constantly constructing and reconstructing myself, like I was some useless academic critic.

Still, it seems I'm always asking questions and not pretending to have very many answers.

I wasn't there when Michael Sherwood died in that car wreck. I wasn't. But I was there when he sat on my chest and spat into my mouth for an hour. I wonder, though, if he really spat into my mouth for an hour. Maybe it was just for a few minutes. Maybe he only spat in my mouth once. But no matter how many times he actually spat in my mouth on that particular day, he has spat in my mouth a thousand times since.

That's how our memory works. It does. Our memories repeat over and over like a scratched record. It seems I have too many memories. Is that possible? Can a person have so many memories that they spill out of his head and onto the floor? Can a person have so many memories that they fall out of his car as he's driving somewhere and follow him down the highway forever? Can a person check into a strange hotel and find a lost memory waiting in the room for him?

An Indian's whole life is guided, shaped, and controlled by memory, in a much more tangible way than for most Americans. Maybe it's because Indians still believe in magic. I'm not the only Indian who can't always tell the difference between his dreams and his reality, between science and magic.

What am I trying to say?

My whole life has been about metaphors. You see, when Michael Sherwood sat on my chest and spat into my mouth all those years ago, he wasn't just Michael Sherwood. By now, he has become every Indian boy, my mother and father, my lovers, my own fear and pain, and my own memories. You see, when Michael Sherwood died in that car wreck, he didn't really die. He moved into my house.

Yes.

Michael Sherwood moved into my house, in spirit, in memory. But when his body died, crushed under the weight of his car, I imagine Michael learned something new, something about metaphor. As Michael lay on his back, with that car on his chest crushing the life out of him, I imagine that Michael remembered the time he sat on my chest and spat into my mouth. I imagine he died with the memory of my tears, my face, my pain.

Is that justice? Is there ever justice?

I don't know. I'm only sure about car wrecks and forgiveness. I'm only sure about spit and love.

VI.

Everything is in the first person.

VII.

When I was fourteen years old, my mother and father adopted James, who was actually my second cousin. But my mother and father adopted him because his natural mother could barely take care of herself. So, James my little cousin became James my little brother.

He was malnourished and sickly when he first came into our home. Just a little past one year old, he would drink bottle after bottle of milk. As he grew older, his hunger only increased. When my father and I would stop at 7-Eleven for our ritualistic Big Gulps of Diet Pepsi, James would take a drink from each of our cups. But these were not ordinary drinks. No. James would put his mouth to our straws, draw in a deep breath, and suck that Diet Pepsi up and up and up. James would hold his breath for a minute, for two minutes, and drink and drink and drink.

We laughed at it then. Now, the memory frightens me.

If James was once that hungry and thirsty, would he ever learn to be full and satisfied? No. Would I?

Sometimes I look at James as if he were me. Since he has replaced me in our home on the reservation. I live in Spokane but the rest of my entire family still lives in the same house we all grew up in. My big brother, Arnold, still sleeps in his basement bedroom. My twin sisters, Kim and Arlene, still share a bedroom next to my parents' room. When it's too hot or cold in their own rooms, my sisters and mother all still sleep on mattresses thrown onto the living room floor, while my father sleeps through everything. And James sleeps in his room across the hall from Arnold's. James sleeps in the room that used to be mine.

In fact, even though the walls are covered with James's heroes, and his comic books and Nintendo games are scattered around, the whole family still refers to the room as mine. When I spend the night out on the reservation, I sleep in "my" room and James joins the women on the living room floor.

When I am not there at home on the reservation, which is most of the time, James sleeps in my room. He sleeps in the same position I used to sleep in at his age: slightly fetal, with his hands tucked between his thighs for warmth. All these years later, I still wake up from night-mares in that position. What does James think when he wakes up in that position?

It would be easy here for me to assume I know James's thoughts. Isn't that what writers are supposed to do, jump into other people's heads and learn them? Move them around like puppets? Predict their every movement and emotion? But I don't know what James thinks or feels unless he tells me what he's thinking or feeling. Even then, James is only telling me a carefully edited and/or random version of what he's thinking and feeling.

There it is. I don't know James all that well, even though he and I have similar features, both get too many nosebleeds, both have a bad right eye, and both cry ourselves into sickness whenever our feelings are hurt. My family tells us that we are so much like each other that it's scary.

I'm never quite sure what they mean.

I do know that writers like to jump into the heads and hearts of "others," of their fictional characters. I suppose I could jump into James's life and "inhabit" him. I love to read how good writers "in-habit" their characters. I love to read that because it proves how redun-dant most criticism can be. Of course, all writers, good or bad, inhabit their characters simply because writers are their characters. All those people running around in our poems, our stories, our novels, our es-says are merely little parts of us dressed up in masks.

Writers are always just writing about themselves.

Maybe that's what upsets me most when white writers use Native American material. A white writer is not Native American and never will be, no matter how hard they try. I read in *People* magazine that Barbara Kingsolver feels like an Indian in her bones. No. She doesn't feel Indian in her bones. You can't feel Indian in your bones unless, of course, you are an Indian.

When Kingsolver finishes writing about Indians, she gets up from her typewriter and she's still white. When I'm finished writing this essay about being Indian, I have to go out and buy some groceries, as an Indian.

This all brings me back to James.

Once, my whole family sat and watched some goofy movie on television. James and I shared a couch and halfway through the movie we both got bloody noses. Really. Our noses started to bleed at the same time and the rest of our family laughed and screamed in shock.

"It's like you are the same person," they said.

No. James and I are not the same person. We are both separate, distinct, and beautiful. Maybe we share some strange sort of bond, but we cannot be combined into the same image.

There is evidence. Photographs. In one such photograph I'm playing basketball with James and his best friend, John. If you look closely you can see that James and I are not the same person. If you look closely you will see that James and I are both Indian, and he and I don't need a photograph or book to know what that means.

VIII.

My name is Sherman Alexie and I'm an alcoholic. [Read from cue card that says "Hello, Sherman!"] I've been sober for _____ years and _____ months. [Insert applause here] I just want you to know that I take it day by day, you know? [Stand for ovation here]

I didn't take my first drink of alcohol until I was eighteen years old and I took my last drink of alcohol when I was twenty-three years old. In between, I drank so much that I sometimes believed I was invisible.

It's pretty easy to be flippant about the whole affair now. I was simply one of those Indians upholding our stereotype, right? I was just another drunk Indian standing on the highway and screaming at all the cars that passed him by. Well, I was a drunk Indian and did spend one crazy night standing on a deserted highway and screaming at all the stars that laughed at me. I didn't even have the luxury of screaming at one car.

So what does this mean?

I am an adult alcoholic. I was a child in an alcoholic family. But I'm not an adult alcoholic just because I'm an Indian, and I wasn't a child in an alcoholic family just because it was an Indian family. There are many reasons for all of it. In fact, some of the reasons for my alcoholism probably sound like the reasons that other people are alcoholics, no matter what color they are.

Let's be real: Indians aren't the only alcoholics in the world. I know everybody reading this essay is either an alcoholic or has had their lives directly affected by an alcoholic. Right?

It seems to be that Indians get the alcoholic label, though, because we usually pay less for our drinks. I mean, what's the difference between an Indian wino drinking Thunderbird wine in the alley and a business executive drinking three martinis at lunch? The price of the drink and the color of their skin.

That said, I wonder how this alcoholic stereotype affects the critical interpretations of my work. I know all of the reviews of my book of short stories, *The Lone Ranger and Tonto Fistfight in Heaven*, focused on the alcoholics in the book. Yet none of the reviewers mentioned or noticed the fact that all of the major male characters in the book have never drunk or have stopped. The reviewers also failed to notice, shockingly, that none of the major female characters drink. Lester FallsApart is the only character in any of my work, poetry or fiction, who continues to be an active alcoholic and refuses to do anything about it.

Yet I must consider the fact that I am a recovering alcoholic writer. Does my own alcoholism infuse the pages of my books with my former and current desperations? Do all those critics and readers out there have these incredibly sensitive noses that can sniff out the minute traces of cheap beer forever imbedded in my fingertips? Do they know? Do they look at my author's photo and see the man who passed out a hundred times on his favorite chair, with a half-empty cooler of beer on the floor beside him?

Do you know me?

IX.

I consider myself a deeply spiritual person. I am influenced by my own tribal heritage and by Christianity. I consider myself a Spokane/Coeur d'Alene Christian. I believe in God. I believe in Jesus Christ and who he was, and, more importantly, who he is now. I have a deep faith in the idea of heaven. I do not, however, have much faith in Christians.

Above all, remember this: Jesus Christ has dark skin.

X.

I write constantly. I have published five books in the space of nineteen months. I am prolific. I am, as Reynolds Price said in a review of my work in *The New York Times Book Review* (October 17, 1993), "employing [my] gift at a brisk pace." That comment seems like a very condescending view of the volume of my output, but I can't argue very logically with it. I can't argue because I'm not sure why I'm writing with such fervor.

A friend wrote a letter (which went unpublished) to *The New York Times Book Review* regarding the Reynolds Price review, which read, in part,

Sherman Alexie's urgency is one of his strengths. On reservations, the life expectancy of a Native American male is significantly less than that of the average white male. Reynolds Price should consider that a Native American writer may well have reason to feel a greater urgency to write than the average white male "who does not mature until 30 . . ."

I am much more haunted by my friend's letter than by the review. I find myself touching my body, searching for tumors, and worrying about even the slightest of imperfections. I drive more carefully. I constantly check my mirrors, hoping I can avoid the car wreck that is supposed to kill me. I try not to use my word processor if there's an electrical storm raging outside.

But no matter how often my imagined and real fears threaten to overtake me, I still hear the poems and stories in my head. In the end, those poems and stories are themselves not afraid. Those poems and stories rage and roar, whisper and sing, dance and drum.

Maybe I write so hard because I'm afraid of death. Maybe I write so hard because I'm so much in love. Maybe I write so hard because I'm Indian. Maybe I write so much because most of you are white.

I don't know exactly why I write. I don't pretend to know. I won't lie about that. I won't tell you a magical and tragic tale that explains everything. I don't know the moral of this story. But I do know that my fingers are hot and sore after a few hours of typing, of pushing my words into a computer's memory.

I know this. I know this. I know I have so much left to say and I don't know how much time I have left to say it all.

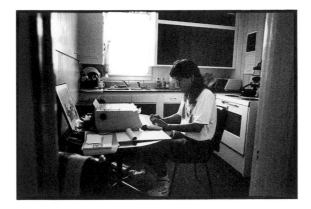

SHERMAN ALEXIE tells the truth through his poetry and fiction. That truth encompasses love and self-esteem, as well as the pain, racism, and acts of hate that are part of life for him and his fellow Native Americans. He is a young man in a hurry to tell his stories.

◊

Alexie was born in 1966 in Spokane, Washington. He grew up in Wellpinit, on the reservation outside Spokane, and went to school there until his high school years, when he bused thirty miles each day to a school off the reservation. "I could have gone to any school, but I just needed a better one than the tribal school," he remembers. "As a kid I was picked on. They said I was an apple (red on the outside, white on the inside) and a geek. I had those government-issue glasses.

"I was sort of Catholic, and I was going to be a doctor," Alexie says. "I was on that academic track until I attended Gonzaga University [a small Catholic college in Spokane with about 2,500 students]. I attended the school for two years and had problems. Then I transferred to Washington State University in spring 1988, looking for a big public school and more of a chance to be anonymous."

At WSU, Alexie met Alex Kuo, a poet and faculty member teaching creative writing, who encouraged him

to develop his writing talent. He had written journals when he was at Gonzaga, but his first assignment in creative writing class was to write five poems, something he had never done before. Reading those poems, Professor Kuo asked him if he had ever considered becoming a writer. The poems in *The Business of Fancy-dancing* were drawn from assignments in Kuo's class.

Alexie explains, "I hadn't been reading any other poets, so I took a crash course in contemporary poetry. I especially read the Native American writers like Ray Young Bear, who is in Iowa." Others whose work he studied were Simon Ortiz, Joy Harjo, James Welch, Leslie Silko, and Adrian C. Louis.

"I was going to graduate from WSU in American Studies, but as a protest against the school I got close but never graduated. After getting 200 poems published in my years there, I never got any recognition or attention, no positive gestures at all. Some faculty members there were good, but there is a lot of conservative ignorance politically and socially at that school," Alexie contends.

Alexie worked for People to People, a nonprofit organization in Spokane, for nine months as program information coordinator. That turned out to be the only "real job" in his life; the next year, 1992, he received a National Endowment for the Arts fellowship, and after that, book contracts.

◊

Alexie has become highly visible on the literary circuit. Between January 1992 and August 1993, he gave eighty-two readings from his first three books of poetry. This was before the big publicity push in the fall of 1993 for his first book of short stories, *The Lone Ranger and Tonto Fistfight in Heaven*. He has given readings in many parts of the United States, at colleges and in bookstores, and has been featured on National Public Radio's "Fresh Air."

"I'm going to a lot of places where there is no visible Native American population, like New York City and L.A.," he says. "It was interesting at New York University; there were sophisticated people with many ideas about Native Americans, but they thought Spokane was a suburb of Seattle.

"A lot of the time I meet people whose conception of Indians comes from New Age literature," Alexie complains. "I often meet men's-movement types who think that I'm supposed to have a real spiritual background. I turn down offers I receive to speak at their conferences."

The identity of Indian men, however, is something that Alexie has given a lot of thought. Some Indian men he meets "still have the warrior mentality, but there is nothing left to hunt. This mentality is still big in tribes. At every powwow there is the veterans' dance, where the U.S. military veterans or their widows or mothers

perform a special dance. The Vietnam vets are a big thing. There is so much military fervor among Native tribes." To Alexie, the time for that warrior fervor is past; it is antiquated thinking. "I think there should be substitute models for young men—take up writing or another career, be a warrior plumber."

◇

Sherman Alexie is a recovering alcoholic, now practicing total abstinence. His father was an alcoholic, never abusive but often absent. "When he was there, he was nurturing and very domestic; he was responsible for child care," Alexie remembers. "Mom was alcoholic too, but she was also the breadwinner—she worked as a counselor. She quit drinking because she got tired of it."

As an eighteen-year-old student at Gonzaga, he became a bingeing alcoholic for what he terms "genetic and cultural reasons. I was an alcoholic from the ages of eighteen to twenty-three," he notes, adding that his addictive behavior probably was due to cultural stress, not being with his people, and not having a positive concept about them. "I finally just quit because I got tired of it and also because I realized as I gained more success in my writing, it was not a good role model for Native youths. I realized that when I was drinking, my skills would diminish. I also would get sick on it."

Alexie points out that he's the only one of his family to live off the reservation. His family includes an older brother who works in a bingo parlor, twin sisters who work in the health field for the tribe, and a younger brother whom Alexie tries to visit often.

"I was the one shut in my room reading all the time, but I think they can visualize my life now. They are proud and happy for me in my successes.

They all made sacrifices to get me to college; they all worked and paid for me. I think my family tolerates my extreme honesty about my past in my books," he states. "They recognize the need to be honest but also figure, 'That's just him, being Junior.'"

Alexie's future is dedicated to writing. "I'm going to write until I get tired of it, until I have to quit, but right now I don't think there is anything else that would interest me." However, he is beginning to pursue other forms of expression that stem from writing. He has collaborated with musician Jim Boyd, a Colville Indian, and has talked about making his stories into movies. He has also pursued theatrical presentations of his work and has developed and performed a dramatic monologue about a Native man, Lester FallsApart.

He is pleased but puzzled by the uniformly positive reviews of his work. "There hasn't been a bad review, but then they don't know how to review my work. Some are off—they don't really understand my point of view." Nonetheless, Alexie is not complacent. He is not satisfied with his writing yet and feels it could be a lot better. "Maybe in a few more years it'll get there," he remarks.

Though the setting for his books is the dramatic desert and rock of eastern Washington, there is no physical description of the locales in his poems and writing. He remarks that it's the interior landscape that is important to him and figures that nature can take care of itself.

As for his working style, he explains, "I am writing and rewriting continually. I can go twelve to fourteen hours a day for a week. But I am impatient; I go through a lot of stuff and write a lot, then go back through it, maybe doing the same story over. You must write a lot to get one great poem—of 130 poems, maybe there are ten good ones."

Ultimately, Alexie feels, the measure of his success will depend on whether reservation Indians read his books, and understand and like them. "I think my work has been successful because I try to communicate with people who don't normally read poetry. There's more guts and heart than head in my writing. It's visceral."

The War Is Not Over

Tom Spanbauer

1946. The war is over.

We lived in a thin white house my mother tried to round the edges off of, with Virginia creeper, the delphinium, the red Seven Sisters rose turned pink—sun-bleached, my mother said—and the two red geraniums in clay pots by the back door smelling things up. June 30, a water sign, summer, southern Idaho, the desert.

I am.

From the foundation, all the way around the house, out to the cedar posts my mother painted white, was the lawn. The lawn, the green line that was the same as the line of the house out farther. Wire netting to keep us kids in. Not one tree in the yard. A stand of cottonwoods up by the canal, but in the yard no trees, no shade, just the shade edges of the house on the lawn.

The other line was the horizon, out farther from the lawn. After that things dropped off.

The house was smells. Coal oil in the front room. Cookstove, kindling, roast beef and gravy in the kitchen—sometimes pie, coffee. Zeke's Medicated Ointment, my father's boots, Old Spice, Viceroys in the bathroom. All over the house, soap and wet clothes on Monday. Ironing on Tuesday. What else?

The other smells. My father's saddle room in the barn. Horse shit. Our horse Chub. The inside of the old pickup. My mother's cedar jewelry box on her vanity in their room, the smell of the cedar and the red rose from her wedding cake mixed together with her gold band bracelet, and her earrings: the rhinestones, the gold autumn leaves, the Eiffel Tower ones. The smell of the red linoleum in the hallway. The smell on the windows; sagebrush and doily curtains washed in White King soap. Wind on the window glass has a smell. The smell of the wet soapy rag wiping dust. She never could get rid of the dust.

In the winter it was white, all white high over the fence, just white, sky and world white into each other, no line, only the sag of the wires between the crucifix tops of the telephone poles too high for the snow, to Pocatello, to church, the line we drove in the Buick to God.

Another line. The line just on the other side of the fence in front of the house, across the road, at the edge of the barrow pit, the fence there. The reservation. The wire netting to keep them in, not us out. Cut through everything, that line, through America. Those people, everything handed to them, my father said. Sagebrush on that side of the fence. Sagebrush my father wants to plow under. No worth in sagebrush.

One day, me and my sister, it is sunny, so bright I'm still squinting, my sister dares me to pick the flower over there, over the line, where it's the Indians'. I crawl over our fence, cross the gravel road they asphalted that summer, the white line down the middle, to the barrow pit on the other side, to the edge, that fence, netting and two strands of a barbed wire above the netting. I look north and south and east and west, stick my foot into the wire netting at a cedar post, climb up, swing my leg over, down the fence the other side, put my foot on Indian land, stand on both feet, walk on Indian land, their land under my shoes a feeling all the way up to my stomach, walk to the flower, a sun orange and yellow on the rocks, no smell at all. I pick the flower, the cactus flower, run through the sagebrush crying, holding out my palm. Where I crawl back over the fence is the sign: NO TRESPASSING.

◆

Portland was because of Aunt Alma. My mother's red-haired sister who moved to Portland for a reason we didn't talk about. My first journey over the horizon, out of the desert, I am five, to Aunt Alma's in Portland. Aunt Alma's sweater dress that was green and her red hair and her red lips, and her friend Theresa she lived with, a painter. I fell down Aunt Alma's basement steps, looking for the bathroom. Cool, smelled so cool lying on her basement floor in Portland.

There was no sun, no bright above to squint from, round edges, shade, rained all week. All around Aunt Alma's house were bushes and flowers my mother just couldn't get over. So many colors. So many ways for a flower to smell. Trees everywhere. Huge hanging deodaras, flowering plums, avenues of flowering plums and crabapple and dogwood.

And roses, the city of roses.

Everything so old-looking, my mother said, the way you see in pictures, like France with old stone bridges and stone staircases that fan out, the lampposts, and the railing you lean against to look down at the river, as if you were looking at the Vatican, or Paris.

The escalator at Meier & Frank, the popcorn we smelled and bought on the street. The drive to the ocean, the road a tunnel through trees.

Cannon Beach. We park, everyone feeling like at Christmas, just over the line of sand dune, the ocean. Then there it is, the ocean, so big my father won't look and goes back to the car. I'm not like him. I can't stop looking. Everything smells wet and cool. The ocean sounds the same as wind in sagebrush and the cottonwoods. Sometimes the wind stops, though, but the waves never stop.

Then my clearest memory yet. From a cabin under a pine tree, a woman walks out of the cabin with a blue pail, the screen door shuts behind her. She is lanky and is wearing a flowered dress. The woman tosses the water onto the sand and walks back into the cabin, the screen door. There is a huge black rock in the ocean. Seagulls. My mother takes my hand. I walk back to the car with her, I look back as I walk, to the ocean, the rock, the seagulls. In the car, I ask about God. Who He is.

Aunt Alma, my mother, my father, my sister, and I go to a seafood restaurant. My mother is wearing lipstick. I'm wearing my Sunday clothes and sit next to Aunt Alma. We eat fried shrimp that ain't frozen. Fish not on Friday. Fresh fish. Aunt Alma smells of Midnight in Paris. I don't know this about Midnight in Paris until I'm as old as Aunt Alma was then. I'm junking in a junk shop in Sellwood in Portland, and I open a little, dark blue bottle, Midnight in Paris. I smell the blue bottle and in the bottle is the ocean and a lanky woman tossing a pail of water.

◆

In Africa, in the Peace Corps, I live in a tent on the savannah, a world so flat the horizon is a line around me forever. One day, I stand on a huge black rock and watch the thunderclouds. Rain flattens the grass toward me, a world so flat you can see the edge of the rain. Twenty feet from me the grass is flat. Ten. I hold out my palms. The edge of the rain is on my palms, elbows, my shoulders. I am drenched in a second.

Outside my tent is an anthill shaped like an enormous red penis. The shadow from the enormous penis out farther. The earth is red sand. When I build my round mud house in the desert, I haul the water from a pipe two miles away. Each morning an old Masai stands under the only tree for miles and watches me work. When my house is finished, he approaches me. We greet each other. He is naked, smells of cow manure, leather gourds filled with goat milk. I make tea.

One thing, the old man asks, I'd like to know. Why did you build your house in the river? he asks. I look around to the red dust blowing in the wind, up at the tree, at my house in the low spot under the tree. What river? I ask. He points his long finger into the dust we're sitting on. His finger is a sundial, the shadow. This river, he says.

◆

In New England, up north, the low hardwood valleys push my eyes to the road. I speed by history, the border of granite fences, to a life carved out of stone. The locals are Scotch-plaid, self-sufficient, important individuals, transcendentalists. Winter is their only excess.

There is a photograph of my seasons in New Hampshire. In the drawer that smells of glue and wax, the photograph is in with the staples, the ruler, the Viceroys, and the speaker wire.

Good fences make good neighbors.

A flatlander, I did not live free, and died.

◆

Down South, in Key West, the sun set faster than my visual purple. Shadows are heavy black things you can fall in. Everyone wears lavender.

The sun has bleached us, baked out the primary. The island so small there's no horizon of it. The horizon has vaporized, and what isn't is more than what is.

Beneath my lavender kimono I am transparent, and all my friends are drunk. Smelling cocaine. I disrobe and dive into swimming pool blue. There is a flash: one solid, silent thrust.

I get pinkeye from the pool. My eyes are red like in Idaho baling hay, like in Kenya dust storm savannah. I rub my eyes. Scratch the cornea.

That day the sun is a bright knife. I walk, my hands over my eyes, one step at a time, my feet in the direction I think is the hospital. Wind in the royal palms. Midday it is midnight, a heavy black thing I am fallen into. All my friends are dying. Their funerals smell of roses.

◆

In New York City, America's dark basement, I've fallen and I can't get up. On Forty-Third Street, I plant a tree in front of my window. The tree dies. I plant another tree. The tree dies. A fine black dust covers my apartment, the day after I dust. The windows smell of cigarette. One night I wake up. Summer, hot and sticky. A woman is screaming in the hall. Midnight in Manhattan, I open my door, don't unlatch the chain. Neon light from above makes me squint. So big you can't look. The woman is naked and crack-blind, on the floor with a blue pail. She is splashing water onto herself. She is kicking the walls. The sound from her, her mouth saliva-stretched, the scream I know. I cross a line in me you never want to cross.

When the woman in the hall stops, I step over her and go out. The pail is empty. Under my shoes, a feeling all the way to my stomach. The only thing that helps is walk. Outside, I look North, South, East, West.

In Times Square, next to *Chicks with Dicks,* in the middle of the war zone, at the police station made up cute for tourists—a Broadway-show sheriff's office—a Native American man is bloody, for a reason we don't talk about, handcuffed.

The cop's white horse is tethered to a wire netting fence. I jump on the white horse and ride into the horizon, back home. Out West. Through the desert sun to where it's wet. I buy a house, thin, white, surrounded by cottonwoods, in Portland. The windows smell of dry rot and Oregon clay. I dye my hair red and wear lipstick, remodel, try and round the edges off. Round steps that fan out, a round window.

Only rain. I tear up the lawn and plant trees, flowering plums, crabapple, dogwood, and flowers I just can't get over: delphiniums, a red Seven Sisters rose, Virginia creeper. Live with a painter, an African

American, talk about it, him. Talk about the L.A. riots, the Oregon Citizens Alliance, religious fundamentalism, sexual trespass, AIDS. The war.

1993. The war is not over.

♦

I drive to Cannon Beach, buy a blue pail. The huge black rock is a shadow. I think about God, the Great Mystery the same line as me out farther.

I am.

Who am.

I hold my palms out. Pour water from the pail over my eyes. Promise to move to Paris. The waves, I can't stop looking.

What else? Over the Cascade mountains, not far—even in my old pickup, not far—is the desert, dry, flat, where things drop off. Don't fence me in, no NO TRESPASSING signs—out farther where what isn't is more than what is. Beneath my Nike outfit I am naked. Under my boots a feeling all the way to my stomach, my feet in the direction I think is my life. North, South, East, West. The only thing that helps is walk. And the sagebrush.

Smells like God, sagebrush.

At forty-six, **TOM SPANBAUER** is a tall, somewhat shy and quiet man eager to listen to others. His quest has brought him to the understanding that, to write, he also must listen intensely to his heart—something antithetical to his conservative upbringing in Idaho, but more necessary than ever to a gay writer in America.

◊

Spanbauer was born in Pocatello, Idaho to a German Catholic farming family that lived in a deeply Mormon community. "I had an odd sense of myself—I asked, 'What is wrong with me?'" he says. "Being an outsider, taking the bus a long ways to get to Catholic school, I got beat up a lot."

He began writing when he was in grade school. "The nuns encouraged me to write, but not to listen to my heart. I had a few good English teachers, a diary, and a group of bad poems I wrote." Spanbauer eventually earned a degree in English literature at Idaho State University, where he became, ironically, the perfect picture of the active, popular kid.

During the Vietnam War era, Spanbauer spent two years in Kenya with the Peace Corps. "I was not a tourist; I spoke Swahili seventy-five percent of the time. I lived in a tent at the base of Kilimanjaro and vaccinated cows," he remembers. "My job was to be an agent of change, to westernize the natives—and to get them to wear pants. After the first year, I went to Nairobi to supervise the construction of a workshop for jewelry and dress-making; I think the building is still standing," he says with pride. "But there was such a color barrier—it was arrogant to think I could help them. It took me a long time to finally understand a joke."

Spanbauer met Mike Taylor, the African-American artist who would later become his lover and housemate, in Africa during his Peace Corps days. Taylor was teaching art at the University of Kenya. They would meet again and link their lives many years later in New York.

Upon returning to the United States, Spanbauer worked as a social worker and adviser to Native American students at Idaho State University. It was the first time he he had become close to Native Americans, although as a child he lived for years across the road from the Fort Hall Indian Reservation. Spanbauer developed a deep and enduring friendship with a Shoshone colleague, Clyde Hall.

From 1972 to 1978, Spanbauer was married and lived briefly in a commune in Oregon. After short stints teaching high school and working as a landscaper, he became a waiter (a profession he would follow for ten years), left his wife, and went to New England. He took a pivotal life step when he came out as gay at the age of thirty-three. He also began his first novel, describing his life between his wedding and his divorce. Then he moved to Key West for three years. It was a wild time. "I finally got tired of it," he remembers. "There's only so much you can say about suntans and blow jobs."

Spanbauer headed to New York, bringing his manuscript with him. He entered the writing program at Columbia University and for two years he

studied with the excellent faculty. But soon he owed so much money that he had to take a job as a super for six buildings on East Fifth Street. He cleaned sidewalks, took care of garbage, and fixed boilers in return for a free apartment. He was writing all the time and published some short stories, "Sea Animals" and "Mr. Energy."

In 1986, Putnam published Spanbauer's first manuscript as *Faraway Places*. A portion of *The Man Who Fell in Love with the Moon* earned him a contract with Atlantic Monthly Press and the novel was published in 1990.

The Man Who Fell in Love with the Moon was developed from a trip to visit family and friends in an old gold mining town. There, Spanbauer discovered a story about a local prostitute who had died. The novel follows the life of the prostitute and her "family," others who crossed genders, sold sex, and fought the town's Mormon establishment. "I wanted to write it from the point of view of an odd guy, an innocent, a hybrid—not hetero and not gay at first," Spanbauer remarks. "I wanted to explode old myths and forms of gay literature but needed to develop my own language to talk about sex and incest.

"The book was well accepted, but I told my parents not to read it. They are provincial; they read the good reviews and are proud of me, but don't know much about me," he says. "During the L.A. riots they even told a friend of mine 'Tom must be down there in the middle of those riots.' When I visited with my partner, Mike, the nicest thing my mom could think of to do for him was to rent the video *Sister Act*."

Spanbauer's new novel, *In the City of Shy Hunters,* is about an innocent from the Northwest, the open frontier, caught in Manhattan. "He stutters, he is thirty, and he gets an

education right in the middle of the beginning of the AIDS crisis.

"Writing a story is like wrestling with an angel," Spanbauer explains. "If I work hard and beat him, he'll give me a gift of a character—it's not just me creating the characters. The more time I spend with him, the more chances he'll take me to a place I need to be." He feels that each of his characters has a new language, and each word of the book is in the language of that character: "Each word has that character wrapped around it."

Spanbauer's books address controversial racial and sexual issues. For example, in *The Man Who Fell in Love with the Moon*, the figure of Berdache is a Native American man-woman, a sacred spiritual leader. "I teach a course in dangerous writing," he says, "about going someplace in yourself that is risky and scary to you. This is what gives your work gravity—you need to make the investment of psyche and soul, find the places you haven't looked at yet. Then you're not *People* magazine. Your success is based directly on how much you open yourself up." He says he can't think about or read other authors very much because it might take his attention away from his own writing. "I need to protect my own self and my own thing—it's very tenuous and scary, this thing you do with yourself. I'm always questioning whether I'm going to get my spirit up to write each day."

Despite his new fame, Spanbauer worries about his future income and questions whether he wants to take a university teaching position, "babysitting rich white kids." *The Man Who Fell in Love with the Moon* has been optioned for a movie, and he has received an advance for his next novel. A resident of Portland, in 1994 he spent six months in Spain in a writing residency sponsored by the University of Barcelona.

Coming from a Soulful Place

Lawson Fusao Inada

I. CLOCKING

I clocked it—about a half hour. Or, I left the house at dusk, and still had enough light to set up camp when I got there. A mountain lake, the run of the place. And then along came a distinguished porcupine, nosing about, shuffling along, taking its holy time. Some deer danced by, doing what does do, a fawn does, passing the buck. By then I had a campfire going, smoke rising through wafting firs, sparks climbing to meet the stars . . .

II. FURTHER CLOCKING

Since 1966, I've been situated about ten minutes from California, according to borders. It takes me about the same time (eight hours) to get to Fresno or to Seattle, to the Bay Area or Portland (five hours), while to get to the concentration camp site at Tule Lake takes about an hour (and fifty years).

My job got me here, and I'm grateful every day (amazed, actually) to have it—to be earning my living as a professor of English. (My late grandparents sit in back of each class, nudging one another, whispering intrusively in Japanese.) My wife and I long ago decided to settle here, to raise our family, and, with my "woodshed mentality" (as in Charlie Parker "woodshedding" with Lester Young records in the Ozarks), I've had ample opportunity to do just that—in a basement, a garage, a barn, and now in my own outback study.

It's modest, it's humble, it's home.

III. NORTHERN LEANINGS

My second Northwest home is Portland, where I often go to share my work and visit colleagues like poet Vern Rutsala (a friend since 1960 in Iowa) and pianist Andrew Hill, composer of the "American Nikkei Symphony" (I wrote the liner notes for his latest release).

Moreover, it has been my privilege to serve on two recent Portland projects. The Japanese American Historical Plaza includes Issei (first-generation) poetry and mine, etched in stone beside the Willamette River (it's a thrill to observe the effects of our verse—from an *unburied* position!). Then there's the new, traveling exhibit, "In This Great Land of Freedom: The Japanese Pioneers of Oregon," with my words in the accompanying catalog—"poetic captions" alongside wonderful historic photos. I feel very much a part of the greater Nikkei (Japanese heritage) community, which, as I've been finding recently, has a considerable and remarkable tradition in poetry.

IV. TREES, SEEDLINGS

American poetry, written in Japanese, going back to about 1910, when on the East Coast Robert Frost, Ezra Pound, and William Carlos Williams first started publishing. Here, the poetry forms were *haiku* (a form that provided vision to Pound and Williams, and continues to be a considerable force in international poetry today) and *senryu* (similar to haiku, but with more "human nature" than "nature" alone).

Ryuko (her senryu name) Saito, the leader of Portland's senryu group (they meet on a monthly basis and publish a booklet bimonthly, along with holding an annual conference in either Tacoma, Seattle, or Portland), is eighty-three, and began composing senryu in 1936, whereas Jonan Kinoshita, a relative beginner, wasn't compelled to start writing his poems until 1942, when he found himself interned in the Portland Assembly Center and assisting at the bedside of Honda Sensei, the master and founder of American senryu, who imparted his teachings on this poetry form before dying.

So Mr. Kinoshita composed senryu all through the camp years (it's interesting to think of writing poetry behind barbed wire, which says something about poetry, and priorities) and on into the present. Here's a recent poem, translated:

> Even with naturalization
> the spirit of the Meiji Era
> does not disappear.

Which figures, since he's ninety-seven.

And since Kinoshita means "beneath the tree," you can see where I, a seedling poet, stand in the tradition of Northwest poetry.

V. ONE HAND CLAPPING

At a recent social gathering in Portland, I was introduced to Mrs. Shiogi, who is the leader of a semiactive and longstanding haiku group. So, the next time, I'd love to meet with them. I figure they could teach me a few things about poetry and life. Mrs. Shiogi is 102, while others in her group are only at the century mark. The smile on my face: one hand clapping!

VI. COMING FROM

Now, while I live where I live—geographically, appreciatively—I'd like to use this opportunity to share some thoughts about where I really live, or where I'm coming from, that is, my inner landscape: places that stay with me, wherever I am; places that provided me with vision, affirmation, and aspiration (in the sense that I aspire to be like the people in those places—generous, warm, strong).

As with anyone, I've been blessed by experience (including the concentration camp experience, which, in its own way, was very *soulful*), and there isn't enough space for me here to acknowledge all those who have treated me "like family." However, beyond my immediate and rather extended family (we're rather "tribal" people), there are two families that really were family to me (my high school graduation picture prominently displayed alongside their own children), and I simply want to share them with you—because they're a large part of me.

VII. "LA BAMBA"

After the war, we lived for a while at my grandparents' home (the home and family fish store were entrusted to longtime friends, German and Italian families), on "E" Street in West Fresno, but my father picked peaches and grapes, resumed his dental practice, and rented us a house on Collins Avenue, several blocks away.

The very first day, I simply went across the street to play, at the Palomino home, with their boys my age—and, for the next decade or so, all through grade school, high school, and college, there were very, very few days when I *wasn't* at the Palominos'. They had five children, and I, an only child, became the sixth; thus, they even gave me my own name: at first, Grandmother called me "Losano," but little sister Sylvia said I was "Chano"—as I am to this day.

Now let me try to describe that *soulful place*. Well, in a very real sense, the entire West Side was *soulful*—in contrast to the nameless and rather generic "other side" of the Southern Pacific tracks. It was just there, like anywhere, pretty much undistinguished, whereas on the West Side, or just in our neighborhood, you could travel and be somewhere in a few seconds: China, Japan, the Philippines, Mexico, Germany, Italy, Mississippi, Armenia, a Basque province, Slavic lands, and so on around the world (including America before Columbus).

You get the picture. And while I'm not saying that elsewhere was *soulless*, *soulful* was very much a West Side term, coming from the black community. And I think you just have to *feel* it—like drowsing off to sleep on a summer night with blues and mariachi music drifting through your window from the bars and outdoor cantinas of Chinatown, as we called our business district. Blues and *mariachis*—and sleep . . .

Sometimes we'd sleep outside on the Palomino lawn, and talk, and dream, and listen. On summer days, we'd just sit around in the shade of the "summer kitchen," a sheltered area in the backyard, and just watch: Grandmother making soap, women making tortillas and cooking corn, cactus, chiles, squash, beans, tomatoes, whatever else was in the garden. And I could always, always, stay to eat. And maybe go to mass later, with the family.

Such small things were huge to me, not simply because I needed them, coming out of camp, but because the family really was special, and their home very definitely was and is a *soulful place*.

VIII. "SWING LOW . . ."

When the Jones family settled in across the street from my grandparents, my academic career rapidly advanced. In grade school, I just listened to the music—a lot. But in junior high, Sam Jones and I began to seriously study it—and his home became our true academy.

We had most of our classes together on through high school, and we did well in them, as a matter of course; but his home held most of the challenge and excitement, because it was the "home of the music." And music was the true curriculum of school anyway, as evidenced by what the students listened to and played on their own: blues, rhythm and blues, jazz (Bird and Pres were household words to the multicolored student body).

What made Sam's home special was the history it contained; whereas all the hip West Side jukeboxes in bars, barber shops, restaurants, pool halls, and shine parlors had a full range of the music from gospel to bop, the Jones collection spanned decades, not just the latest, and was an invaluable archive and library, a major resource, a repository. So as I visited my grandparents, which was often, I also went to study at the Jones classroom.

The front room, where the old phonograph was—where much of the collection was stacked. All fragile 78s, of course, which the family had seen fit to carry from the Deep South. (Which says something, again, about priorities; come to think of it, I remember hearing the family say "carry" often, along with "child.") Now, since Mr. Jones was a minister, the music was just about all "sacred" (which of course contained any number of brilliant and astounding musical styles).

For "secular" music, Sam would steal into his older brother's room, where there was another phonograph, and bring out another stack of platters. And while everyone was out working, he'd mix them and we'd listen, going from a vintage version of, say, "Swing Low, Sweet Chariot" to Dizzy's "Swing Low, Sweet Cadillac," carrying on all the while—laughing, talking, dancing, jiving.

Sure, we were just kids. However, imagine this little scenario: suppose Dr. Music Professor, Ph.D., got a flat tire (hard to believe, because what in the world would he be doing on the West Side?), heard all the ruckus, and knocked on the door (couldn't use a jack, Jack!). He'd find a "colored" boy and an "Oriental" boy listening to music that, as a dedicated musicologist, he'd see fit to inquire about.

"Excuse me, boys, but what's that you're listening to?" "Nothing."
"No, I mean the record that's playing." "'Dewey Square.'" "By?" "Bird."
By his lack of reaction (or overreaction, like jotting down notes), we'd
realize the extent of his academic, cultural, and social deprivation; I
mean, we could have said "Johnny Hodges," an obvious lie, and he'd
have believed it! "Sister Rosetta Jones," "T-Bone Inada"—they'd work
as well. This poor guy was as ignorant as our teachers!

I suppose we could have told him, "Come back tomorrow, man,"
but we had other things to do, starting with carefully replacing the
records. Then we'd stroll down "E" Street, past the big Buddhist temple, over to the Lightning Record Company, where the Chinese owner
let us sit in a listening booth for hours. Sometimes he'd "hip" us to
the latest sounds, like Wardell Gray's latest, and discuss what he called
"America's greatest music," which we knew anyway.

Later on, we might go over to Tulare and "G," where Mr. Jones
was preaching on the corner. We'd stand around and listen—Mr. Jones
on accordion, Mrs. Jones on guitar, Little Sister on tambourine. It would
be as beautiful as anything on record.

By then, thanks to Little Sister, the family was calling me "Laws,"
as in "loss," which was certainly my gain. "The House of the Music"—
even a musicologist might consider it to be a reasonably soulful place.

IX. MOMENTUM AND GRAVITY

Boys become men, and something else sets in. So, before long, following a Mexican wedding I attended with the Palomino young men, I
found myself crashing through a muddy vineyard on my way to an
orchard adjoining a labor camp, where a person would meet me under
the moon. She didn't show—and I know her ferocious father and bel-
ligerent older brother had everything to do with that. Which was to be
respected. Or else.

Then, after Sam told me that Miss So-and-So was "interested,"
I'd dress in judo gear on Wednesday nights, bid my folks adieu (I
told them that my football coach suggested that judo would pay off
on the field, which was the truth), and walk several blocks to a hot,
converted shed where mean old sweaty men would politely and delibe-
rately hurt me, tossing me repeatedly to the floor by way of some per-
verse demonstration of momentum and gravity, which I already knew
from school.

After a while, I'd dust myself off, bow, thank them(!), put on my
shoes, and, pleading "homework," trot a few blocks and lean up against
a fig tree, to cool off outside a church. Which, being "fire-baptized,"
was a-rockin' out with some of the hottest, coolest music you ever
heard! When choir practice was over, Miss So-and-So would step out

alone with her radiant self and, hand in hand, we'd stroll to the rural outskirts of town, toward, but not to, her home.

Everything was fragrant and blooming—cotton fields, the moon . . .

Well, it was inevitable, but one Thursday at school she told me that "someone" (it had to be Roy Hines or Joe Slade!) had spotted us under a streetlight, and that, of course, her older brother had jumped on her case about "that no-count Chinaman!" Oh, well. So much for judo. And momentum. And, even then, I understood and respected the gravity of the situation—which is to say, really, now, what would I do if my kid sister was hanging around with some jive dude in a judo suit?

Right. And when you're fifteen, you have to listen to advice. And when you're old enough, you leave (or think you leave) that *soulful place*.

X. COMING FROM

Well, the campfire's getting low. It sure is nice to be here—alone, beside a mountain lake.

LAWSON FUSAO INADA has melded his accomplishments as a poet with a dedication to his community and cultural heritage. A third-generation Japanese American (Sansei), he is perhaps the best-known Asian-American poet, with a long history of publishing and teaching and performing with jazz groups. He also has a quirky, self-effacing sense of humor.

◊

When Inada arrived in Oregon in 1965, he knew nothing about the history of Japanese Americans in the state. He began to learn about their history and became actively involved with Oregon's Japanese-American community on the first Day of Remembrance, held in Portland in 1979 to commemorate the internment of Japanese Americans in concentration camps during World War II.

Later, Inada contributed to other Japanese-American commemorative activities, such as the Japanese-American Historical Plaza, located on newly developed parkland on the shores of the Willamette River in Portland. It was jointly developed by the city and the Japanese-American community.

Inada is proud of his humble roots in America and is close to his family. He was raised with a close-knit extended family, with love, and with music. "My dad was a sharecropper who eventually went to school and

then became a dentist," Inada explains. An only child, he says his father "let me know I should do what I want with my life."

When he started talking of pursuing writing as a profession, he received encouragement from his mother, who had a degree in teaching and who had instructed him in poetry from childhood. "My mother always read the classics of literature to me, and she always saw to it that I had books, even when we were in the concentration camps. My mother is the *real* Professor Inada!"

His grandparents spoke rudimentary English; Inada has written a poem about their knowledge of the important words "cup coffee, piece pie" ("Seven Words of Poetry" in his book of poems *Legends from Camp*).

"They owned a fish market, and after they closed the store, they used to come over and get me out of bed. They would have me perform tap dance, pamper me, take me for rides to see the neon signs in town. I loved to see the trains with them and have ice cream late at night. Their fish market was in Chinatown and everyone knew me; I used to hang out in the bar next door." Inada remembers, "I'd dance and sing there—that was my first interest in music, the power and beauty of music, which I could just *feel* in my body."

◊

Early on, Inada developed a deep appreciation for jazz. In 1942 he was interned with his family in a relocation camp in Jerome, Arkansas. "In camp there was a bachelors' quarters and I used to hang out there. A guy had a record player and he was always playing Duke Ellington's "Mood Indigo." And then my dad was into jazz, too. After we were transferred to the camp in Colorado, Dad went to Chicago to work and he brought back records of Fats Waller and Earl "Fatha" Hines. He had lived on the South Side of Chicago in the black neighborhood. There were nightclubs all over."

Inada studied music in college at Fresno State University, where he played string bass, pursuing classical and then jazz training. He graduated with a degree in English. "When I went to grad school at the University of Iowa Writers Workshop, I took bass lessons, studied, and washed dishes," he says.

"The music has always been in me, which was not unusual because of the access I had to jazz from an early age. I was rather fortunate, actually, because jazz is not just 'entertainment' but a great art form and a major cultural achievement. It's a profound philosophy, a way of wisdom and spirituality; thus, the great ones are among the great visionary forces of our time. So it's been my privilege to collaborate with jazz masters such as Mal Waldron, Marion Brown, Johnny Hammond Smith, and Andrew Hill. I've also performed with some of the leading Asian-American jazz artists, including Russel Baba, Jeanne Aiko Mercer, Mark Izu, Jon Jang, Francis Wong, and members of the band Hiroshima."

◊

Inada has been living in Ashland, in the mountainous south of Oregon, since 1966. After finishing his master's degree at the University of Oregon, he landed an English professorship at Southern Oregon State College in Ashland; he has been teaching there for twenty-seven years. A youthful and handsome man, he hardly looks the professor nearing retirement.

He considers his work a privilege. "I love teaching," Inada says. "Working as a writer can be isolating, but teaching serves to challenge and inspire me,

keep me engaged in an interactive way; in a sense, the classroom is my 'stage' and students are my 'rhythm section.' Heck, if I could afford it, I'd teach for free!"

Inada's wife, Janet, is a fourth- and fifth-grade teacher. His older son, Miles, is a graduate of Yale, and his younger son, Lowell, attended Colum- bia; both returned for further study at the University of Oregon. "Miles is a wonderful visual artist, and Lowell is a heavy philosopher. Janet's a fabu- lous teacher. I type a lot, mow the lawn, and sit in my recliner. But I cook good rice!"

◊

In recent years, Inada has become involved with Tibetan Buddhism. His interest began with the visit of the Dalai Lama's dancers and musicians to the region in 1990. "Their perfor- mance was so moving, and their pres- ence was so humbling and inspiring, that some of us decided to form a meditation group," he explains. "But, since we weren't sure of what we were doing, it was our great fortune that the Venerable Lama Chhoje Rinpoche consented to come

to Ashland to teach us. Thanks to his efforts, we now have a local *sangha*, and he comes up here, or we go down to his Bay Area center, Padma Shedrup Ling, for teachings.

"I'm an ignorant novice, but I know this much: the teachings of Tibetan Buddhism are a magnificent gift to this country. But, lest that sound too serious, let me close with a funny story. When Chhoje Rinpoche first visited us, he wanted to relax with some movies, so I took him to a video place, where he proceeded to select spaghetti Westerns and *The Godfather*. Seeing the puzzled look on my face, he asked me, 'Lawson, what is the difference between an Italian godfather, a Polish godfather, and a Tibetan godfather?'

" 'Uh, I don't know, Rinpoche.'

" 'Well, the Italian godfather makes you an offer you can't refuse. The Polish godfather makes you an offer you can't understand. But the Tibetan godfather makes you an offer you can't refuse *or* understand.' "

To Divine the Hidden

Charlotte
Watson
Sherman

I write out of my fascination with the supernatural—spirits, visions, healing dreams, ancestral memories, blood memories. I write to divine the hidden and am shaped by the Wild West of my imagination. Runaway slaves, Native healers, cowboys, African spiritualists who commune with the dead—all frequent the haunts of the mythical landscape of the Northwest of my imagination.

A writer once told me people were waiting to hear the stories of African Americans living in the Pacific Northwest. I was amazed. I thought I needed to be from Harlem in order to be a writer. I couldn't imagine people interested in a plain, simple place like Seattle. There are no ghettos here, no concrete jungles. Did we have any stories? Was there anything compelling about the presence of African Americans in the Pacific Northwest?

The Kalahari bushpeople believe that a person's story is their most sacred possession, and without a story one doesn't have a nation, a culture, or a civilization. Without a story of one's own to live, no person has a life of their own.

James Baldwin said all writers are writing their own stories, over and over again. Before attempting to explore a collective story, I decided to examine my story, the story of how I came to live and write in the Northwest.

♦

My memory always returns to the photograph. I am five years old and stand on a mound covered with winter flowers. The sky is memory blue. The peak of Mount Rainier is visible behind me. A pointy red cap covers my plaits. My shoulders are hunched, the left one pushed forward as if to protect my body. My royal blue Goodwill coat hangs below my knees. My head is cocked to the right and there is a mask of concentration on my face (no one knew then that I was nearsighted), as if I am trying to see and hear something beyond the frame of the photograph, trying to see something hidden.

My father brought me to this magical place. My father full of magic. And secrets. I look at the photograph and break the spell of my father's secrets. The secret of my father.

My story began before I was born, when my mother, Dot, left Mississippi and rode the train over the Mason-Dixon Line to Washington State. Fresh-faced and twenty-one years old, with the red dust of Louisville, Mississippi, clinging to the edges of her dreams, she came west, seeking the gold of a type of freedom she could imagine, but had never seen.

My mother did not know she was expected, did not know she was to be the hope for my father, his lifeline. She only knew she did not wish to return to the segregation of Louisville or the severe farm of her stepfather, Mr. Ike.

So, with great anticipation for her new life, she descended the steel steps of the sleeping car in which she had traveled for three thousand miles, as if stepping into a dream.

Two weeks after arriving in Seattle, she met a roomer in her uncle's house, the man who was to be my father. His name was Charles, and he was a dapper yellow-skinned man with a disarming smile and a secret.

He was a kind, generous, and mannerable man. A month later they married, and the incessant accusations began. Daily, he accused her of sleeping with men, women, relatives. He spied on her at her job, demanded to inspect her underwear, stood outside her bedroom window at night hoping to catch some imaginary lover in her bed.

Once, after he had started a fistfight with her uncle, he started crying and banging his head against the plate-glass living room window. When he tried to jump through the window, her aunt and uncle took him to Harborview Hospital.

The doctors at Harborview said he was paranoid schizophrenic, but my mother was already pregnant.

When she was five months pregnant, my father slapped her after accusing her of sleeping with her male employer, took all of the money out of their savings account, and returned to his family home in Richmond, Virginia.

The child, my sister, was stillborn. My father remained in Virginia for one year, then returned to Seattle and reconciled with my mother. They were together long enough to conceive another child, me, but the accusations began again. My mother left him, and they divorced before I was born.

It wasn't until after the divorce that my father's relatives told my father's secret: three months before my mother and father met, my father had had a nervous breakdown and ended up in a mental hospital in Washington, D.C. His mother and aunt helped him escape from the hospital, then sent him to stay with his brother in Seattle.

His family had agreed not to tell my mother about the breakdown because they hoped the marriage would change him, would make him better.

No one knew what had caused the nervous breakdown. Maybe it was the brick someone had hit him in the head with during a fight in his youth. Maybe it was caused by his mother not allowing him to marry the girl he had impregnated in Virginia. Or maybe he had been experimented on while he was in the Army during World War II, like those men in the Tuskegee syphilis experiments. No one really knew. This is all part of the secret. And the magic of the unknown.

♦

I look for my sister now in old photographs I hold against the graying light. Sometimes I glimpse her shadow, standing there beside me on a mountain glazed with snow.

I am five with a red scarf wrapped around my throat to stop the chilling winds. Winds that turn my breath to crystals that fall upon my blue Goodwill coat. There is no hood, but a hat sits elflike on my head. Did I say the sky was blue? A rolling sea of blue, a shade I have never seen since.

And there beside me stands the shadow of my sister. My perfect sister. I see her features clearly, even in darkness. Her black eyes are wide-set and oval, her nose a flower, soft and proud. Her lips are the shape my lips make when I smear them with our mother's lipstick and press them to glass, full wet red lips just right for kissing. Her forehead does not wrinkle, even when she is angry. Her skin smooth, flawless. Did I say she was the perfect sister? With hair and teeth some girls would kill for.

I left the warm darkness of our mother's womb headed in the wrong direction. Some would have put me to death, considered me an omen, a sign of something evil. Our mother, strong woman that she is, pushed me from between her thighs; they did not slit her belly to pull me out like fish entrails. If the doctor had not caught me in his gloved hands, I would have landed on the cold tile with my feet flat on the ground.

My sister, of course, slid out the way she was supposed to, perfect head first.

Sometimes I catch myself staring at the sight of two women holding hands. The magic of two women touching. The laughter of connection. The history of memory. I reach for my sister in my dreams, but wake with my hands empty.

If my sister is dawn, then I am dusk. That wild intermingling of seed, our mother and father. She knows them well, the best of each formed her. And me? I got the spare parts. The crescent-shaped scar at the corner of my mouth, the crooked eyes and lopsided smile, the narrow yellow feet.

She knows what to say to our father, who cries, our mother, who is the Great Wall.

The trees on the road leading to my sister stretch naked and grasping toward the steely sky. If I was on foot, I would look just like them. A tall spindly sapling reaching for something outside myself.

This road is lined with gold coins, leaves returning to earth. The next corner will lead to a street that winds like a ribbon into the hills. That is where my sister lives, there at the end of the ribbon, past the iron gate and the stones rising like white mountains into the air. I know exactly where she is, the exact patch of green that is her bed, her resting place. Sometimes I go there and press myself into the damp green. I can almost touch her very bones. The only sounds would be red and yellow leaves falling in a field of whispering green silence, where my sister lies, the only one, my perfect sister born, unborn.

Tell us your stories, the writer said.

◆

A time tunnel. Going back. Home. The center of the world. The core of myself. A sound. Sounds like crying. A man sobbing. My father. One of them. Tears wet his face. It rains here. But not inside. His sobs pierce my little-girl brain. I must save him, but I don't know how. My arms always reach. Out. Like fish lines. Lifelines. I drown sometimes.

I tie my shoes at four. Lace over lace. Entwined. We live with rats. I hate them though they have soft fur. I lay on a mat first time in school. Lullabies try to soothe us. I squirm like a brown wiggly worm. I never am picked to be the good magic fairy. Tapping wands and sprinkling gold dust to those deserving.

I see a car. Big. Shiny. Black. There are lines of these big, black cars and flowers. A flag. Red, white, blue. My mother cries. A man has died. A man she hoped would change things. Slowly. Neatly like whiskey we move across town. A house. Our own. No rats. We have a phone. The number unknown. An old gray woman sends me home from school. In my cotton and lace Goodwill dresses. Down past my knees. The gray one thinks I'll hold the class back. A kindergarten class? Yes. I am black and poorly dressed enough. A lot of power in a four-year-old girl. I stand in corners for laughing. Laughing as they chant the Pledge of Allegiance.

I lie. Tell my pink and Japanese neighbors my mother is a nurse. My aunts—nurses. They don't clean white folks' houses. Though they wear aprons and starchy pressed crisp white and salmon dresses. They are nurses, I say. Nurses. The lie fills my head somehow. Why do I say this? I decide I will be a maid. At six, this is what I will be. And everyone will love me. No, Mommy said. Everyone does not love maids. The only disordered patients my nurse-aunts tend: stacks and stacks, dishes, spoons, cups, glasses. They stand on swollen feet, corns, bunions. In fresh white nursing shoes. Tending pots. Dirty laundry.

I was a girl who loved to run. Head and legs greased, I flew. A young colt with no mane. Three plaits. One cockeyed, I cut it off. With scissors and Joe egging me on. I held it in my hand. Held it to the sun. Smiled. Mommy whipped me with a towel. Her hands. I did not know the importance of hair. It would grow back. She did not care. I got a Curl-Free. The lye burned my scalp. I cried. I tried not to squirm. Or burn my eyes. More hair fell out. In patches and shiny lumps.

I was a cheetah, a gazelle. I ran like black lightning. I was called Zulu. And laughs rang round the playground. I say yes. Yes I am a Zulu. Black and proud. There were only five of us in a sea of pink and gray. And words falling like spears.

◆

I live and write in Seattle because this is where my family lives, my small tribe. I live several blocks from the house I grew up in. My daughters can visit their great-grandmother who lives down the street. They frequently spend time with their grandparents, can touch the living history of their family, that electrical tangle of relationships, and share in our secrets. It is this sense of family and ordinariness that I treasure most about Seattle.

I have listened to a lot of Seattle bashing in my life. Some say this is a place of escape, as far west as you can go and still remain in the United States. My parents did escape the lush but oppressive landscape of Virginia and Mississippi, as did many African Americans who escaped the South as part of the Great Migrations to live on the sacred ground of the Pacific Northwest. Something about the green here reminded them of home.

But I disagree with those who claim that African Americans who ended up in the Northwest lost their sense of African culture. African-isms—those elements of culture with an African origin—transcend geography, space, and time. The people who came here brought with them their stories and superstitions, their quilts and ways of praying, as well as tricks for catching fish—catfish, crappie, bass, bluegill. Though they lived a few thousand miles from their ancestral homes, they did not forget their family ways.

I smile and nod as people from many harried places complain about the strangeness of the people here, about our lack of style, our passivity, our lack of sources of distraction, our weather.

I know they have never sat in a rowboat on the still waters of Lake Kapowsin and cast their line, Mount Rainier ever watchful in the background, or stood at the edge of the world at Neah Bay, as far north and west as you can get and still be in the United States, overlooking water as turquoise as any found at a Caribbean beach.

I wonder if they have ever experienced that particular type of grace, if they have ever taken a deep and full breath and felt themselves connected to the land, felt themselves a part of all there ever was and ever will be.

A fashion disaster, I am grateful for Seattle's grunge, for our lack of all a big city is—its fast life, its despair—and for the smallness of our lives.

The Pacific Northwest is a place for big dreams; the expanse of the land is as wide as my imaginings. Its stop-your-breath physical beauty is both natural and beyond nature. Its sister mountains, primeval islands, and everlasting green are the homes of eternal spirits, the mystical, the unknown. The mythical landscape of the Northwest touches me in the deep places of my dreams.

CHARLOTTE WATSON SHERMAN
is a young African-American writer
dedicated to living and writing in the
Seattle area, and to expanding the
range of literature about her race.
Her stories deal with the dynamics of
families and with the supernatural.

A quiet, conscientious, attractive
woman, she deals with both her family's expectations and the demands of
raising two small children while at the
same time developing a serious writing
career.

◊

Sherman was born and grew up in
South Seattle. Her mother was a cash-
ier and a school bus driver, and her
stepfather worked at Boeing.

"My mother said that I was always
writing and reading as a small child,"
Sherman says. "I read so much, it was
disturbing to them. They said it would
ruin my eyes, that I should get outside
more. When I was ten, a book gave
me the idea that I should try running
away from home. I started walking
up Rainier Avenue and got all the
way up to where Interstate 90 crosses
Rainier Avenue [about seven miles]—
and then my grandmother saw me on
the street with my little suitcase and
called my mom."

Sherman tried to hide her status
as an honor student when she attended the inner-city Franklin High School.
"It was not acceptable to many of
the other African-American youth
to be in the honors crowd," she
remembers.

She chose to attend Seattle
University, a private Jesuit college,
although she was not Catholic, feeling
that a small university was a good
place for her. She took out loans and
worked to pay her tuition. "My parents wanted me to be practical; I majored in social sciences and worked
jobs in criminal justice," she recalls. "I
didn't do well in journalism or English
literature classes, but I still wanted to
be a writer."

A black teacher named Rever-
end Daniels encouraged her to write.
"He even discussed getting me a fellowship to go to England, but I was
scared to go so far away." It was in his
class that she got a sense of the range
of African-American literature.

But the pressure to be "practical"
was still strong. "Although I wanted
to just move to San Francisco and become a writer, I followed others' advice and entered law school at the
University of Puget Sound," Sherman
remembers. "But I found I was unhappy living up to everyone else's
expectations and left after six months.
My parents were crushed, but my
husband was somewhat relieved since
we had a six-month-old baby then."
Her husband, David, was working
full-time in medical technology as an
ultrasound specialist, as well as taking
care of the baby.

Her second daughter was born
in 1985, and Sherman went to work
part-time in the county jail and later
for Seattle Rape Relief.

◊

In 1987, Sherman decided to expand her poetry writing. She had had some pieces published, including three poems in the anthology *Gathering Ground: New Writing and Art by Northwest Women of Color* (Seal Press). With her poems getting longer and longer, she decided to work her way toward fiction.

"I started reading books on how to write, what is fiction, what is a story," she says. "I started by taking a class at the Literary Center, which was a very white situation, even though I'd had a fear of going into a racist situation and feeling vulnerable. In one class a woman started reading from her story, which had many references like 'nigger cats' and 'nigger babies.' I had to leave the room. Later I came back and said that even if she said it was satire it was deeply offensive to me."

Sherman points to a Flight of the Mind writing workshop for women that she attended in Oregon later as a seminal experience. "Ursula LeGuin was teaching this workshop on experimental fiction and it was fabulous. The work was really intensive and a challenge for me."

◇

Her first book of short stories, *Killing Color*, was published by Calyx Books in 1992. That year, she received an individual award from the Seattle Arts Commission and a publication prize from the King County Arts Commission.

"The stories take place in Mississippi, my mother's home, which I had visited with her. The history of the South had a strong impact on me, " she says. "I started writing the stories and it became the first time I thought I had a chance to write the way I wanted to write. The dialect, the extravagant use of language that came out excited me. I started to read other work like that, by other writers introduced to me by my friends Rick Simonson [of Elliott Bay Book Company] and Carletta Wilson [a writer]."

The voices in the *Killing Color* stories were those of Sherman's relatives who had migrated to the Northwest from the South. "Some of them actually don't want their kids to witness the South as they knew it. But after reading my stories, they say *they* have the *real* stories to tell. I love the sound and rhythm of their speech.

"Some people ask me why, in 1993, I write in dialect. Some African-American people are ashamed and don't want to see that past brought to life. They ask, 'Why write about slavery anymore?' I have been told it was a barrier for them to try to read the conversation in dialect.

"I won't sell out," Sherman insists. "It's important to keep a connection to the past because what's happening now, with all the social and behavioral problems in our community, is a direct result of the past. A majority of African Americans have not made peace with that past. There have been no reparations, no monuments, no collective mourning processes. We can't move forward until we have this recognition happen."

It was perhaps a sign of the beginning of that recognition when

Sherman found out that an African-American teen boys group, Rites of Passage, was reading her 1993 novel, *One Dark Body,* about a young woman growing up in the Deep South. "I wrote that book because I think as a race we need a collective rite of passage instead of the gangs filling that void. That they're reading my book is affirming for me, and I feel really honored."

Sherman has recently compiled and edited an anthology of African-American women's writing for HarperCollins. She says she has included about fifteen well-known writers and forty lesser-known writers. "I wanted them all in the book, even though we were way over the page limit," she admits. "There hasn't been something like this for ten years, so I didn't want to leave anyone out, because when will the next opportunity be? The big publishers may have a multicultural commitment now, but how long will it last?"

She is working on her new novel, a contemporary story set in the Northwest. "I was afraid my agent was thinking I should write like Terry McMillan, but that is not the epitome," she says. "African-American writers have a whole range of writing styles.

"At first, coming from Seattle, I didn't think I had the kind of life that would make good writing material. I thought I needed to be from Harlem. I needed to ask the question, 'What is compelling about people in Seattle?' But I decided I can write about ordinary lives of people who live here," she points out. "There is a lot of tragedy and drama in the lives of just folks."

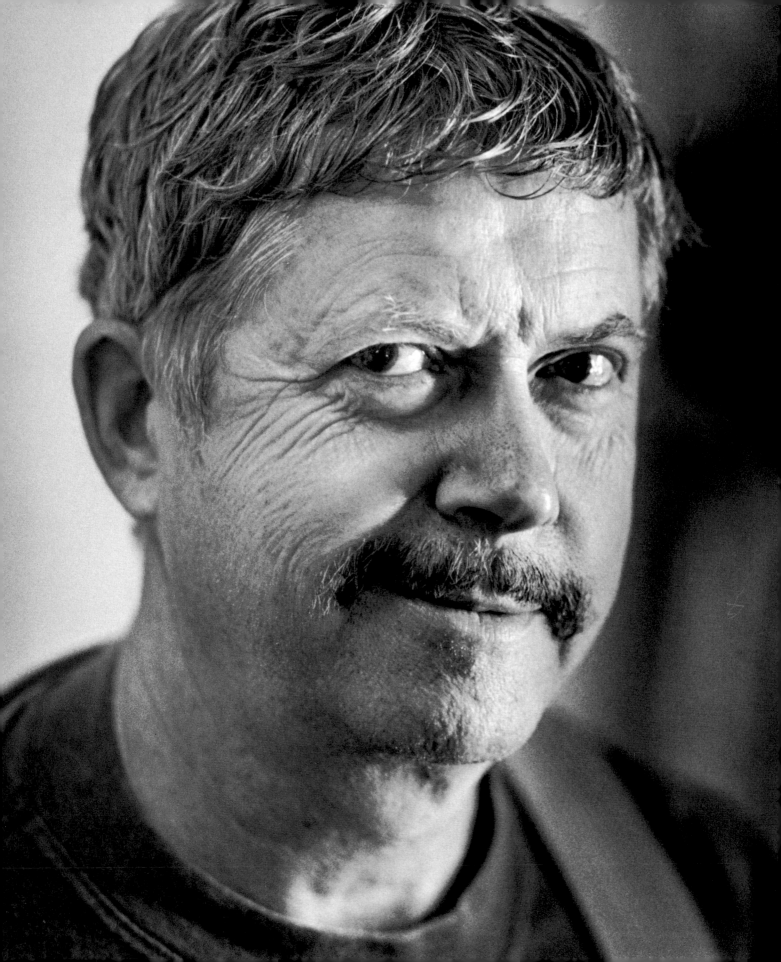

Why I Live in Northwestern Washington

Tom Robbins

I'm here for the weather.

Well, yes, I'm also here for the volcanoes and the salmon, and the exciting possibility that at any moment the volcanoes could erupt and pre-poach the salmon. I'm here for the rust and the mildew, for webbed feet and twin peaks, spotted owls and obscene clams (my consort says I suffer from geoduck envy), blackberries and public art (including that big bad mural the authorities had to chase out of Olympia), for the ritual of the potlatch and the espresso cart, for bridges that pratfall into the drink and ferries that keep ramming the dock.

I'm here because the Wobblies used to be here, and sometimes in Pioneer Square you can still find bright-eyed old anarchists singing their moldering ballads of camaraderie and revolt. I'm here because someone once called Seattle "the hideout capital of the U.S.A.," a distant outpost of a town where generations of the nation's failed, fed-up, and felonious have come to disappear. Long before Seattle was "America's Athens" (The New York Times), it was America's Timbuktu.

Getting back to music, I'm here because "Tequila" is the unofficial fight song of the University of Washington, and because "Louie Louie" very nearly was chosen as our official state anthem. There may yet be a chance of that, which is not something you could say about Connecticut.

I'm here for the forests (what's left of them), for the world's best bookstores and movie theaters; for the informality, anonymity, general lack of hidebound tradition, and the fact that here and nowhere else grunge rubs shoulders in the half-mean streets with a pervasive yet subtle mysticism. The shore of Puget Sound is where electric guitars cut their teeth, and old haiku go to die.

I'm here for mushrooms that broadcast on transcendental frequencies; for Kevin Calabro, who broadcasts Sonics games on KJR; for Dick's Deluxe burgers, closing time at the Pike Place Market, Monday Night Football at the Blue Moon Tavern, opera night at the Blue Moon Tavern (which, incidentally, is scheduled so that it coincides with Monday Night Football—a somewhat challenging overlap that the casual patron might fail to fully appreciate); and I'm here for the flying saucers that made their first public appearance near Mount Rainier.

I'm here for Microsoft but not for Weyerhaeuser. I'm here for Longacres Race Track but not for Boeing. I'm here for the relative lack of financial ambition, the soaring population of bald eagles, and the women with their quaint Norwegian brand of lust. Yes. Ya. Sure, ya betcha.

But mostly, finally, ultimately, I'm here for the weather.

In the deepest, darkest heart of winter, when the sky resembles bad banana baby food for months on end, and the witch measles that meteorologists call "drizzle" are a chronic gray rash on the skin of the land, folks all around me sink into a dismal funk. Many are depressed, a few actually suicidal. But I, I grow happier with each fresh storm, each thickening of the crinkly stratocumulus. "What's so hot about the sun?" I ask. Sunbeams are a lot like tourists: intruding where they don't belong, promoting noise and forced activity, faking a shallow cheerfulness, dumb little cameras slung around their necks. Raindrops, on the other hand, introverted, feral, buddhistically cool, behave as if they live here. Which, of course, they do.

My bedroom is separated from the main body of my house, so that I have to go outside and cross some pseudo-Japanese stepping-stones in order to go to sleep at night. Often I get rained on a little bit on my way to bed. It's a benediction, a good-night kiss.

Romantic? Absolutely. And nothing to be ashamed of. If reality is a matter of perspective, then the romantic view of the world is as valid as any other—and a great deal more rewarding. It makes of life an unpredictable adventure rather than a problematic equation. Rain is the natural element for romanticism. A dripping fir is a thousand times more sexy than a sunburnt palm, and more primal and contemplative, too. A steady, wind-driven rain composes music for the psyche. It not only nurtures and renews, it consecrates and sanctifies. It whispers in secret languages about the primordial essence of things.

Obviously, then, the Pacific Northwest's customary climate is perfect for a writer. It's cozy and intimate. Reducing temptation (how can you possibly play on the beach or work in the yard?), it turns a person inward, connecting them with what Jung called "the bottom below the bottom," those areas of the deep unconscious into which every serious writer must spelunk. Directly above my writing desk there is a skylight. This is the window, rain-drummed and bough-brushed, through which my Muse arrives, bringing with her the rhythms and cadences of cloud and water, not to mention the twenty-three auxiliary verbs.

Oddly enough, not every local author shares my proclivity for precipitation. Unaware of the poetry they're missing, many malign the mist as malevolently as the non-literary heliotropes do. They wring their damp mitts and fret about rot, cursing the prolonged spillage, claiming they're too dejected to write, that their feet itch (athlete's foot), the roof leaks, they can't stop coughing, and they feel as if they're being slowly digested by an oyster.

Yet the next sunny day, though it may be weeks away, will trot out such a mountainous array of pagodas, vanilla sundaes, hero chins, and God fingers; such a sunset palette of Jell-O, Kool-Aid, Vegas strip, and carrot oil; such a sea-vista display of broad waters, firred islands, whale spouts, and sailboats thicker than triangles in a geometry book, that any and all memories of dankness will fizz and implode in a blaze of bedazzled amnesia. "Paradise!" you'll hear them proclaim as they call United Van Lines to cancel their move to Arizona.

They're kidding themselves, of course. Our sky can go from lapis to tin in the blink of an eye. Blink again and your latte's diluted. And that's just fine with me. I thrive here on the certainty that no matter how parched my glands, how anhydrous the creek beds, how withered the weeds in the lawn, it's only a matter of time before the rains come home.

The rains will steal down from the Sasquatch slopes. They will rise with the geese from the marshes and sloughs. Rain will fall in sweeps, it will fall in drones, it will fall in cascades of cheap Zen jewelry.

And it will rain a fever. And it will rain a sacrifice. And it will rain sorceries and saturnine eyes of the totem.

Rain will primitivize the cities, slowing every wheel, animating every gutter, diffusing commercial neon into smeary blooms of esoteric calligraphy. Rain will dramatize the countryside, sewing pearls into every web, winding silk around every stump, redrawing the horizon line with a badly frayed brush dipped in tea.

And it will rain an omen. And it will rain a trance. And it will rain a seizure. And it will rain dangers and pale eggs of the beast.

Rain will pour for days unceasing. Flooding will occur. Wells will fill with drowned ants, basements with fossils. Mossy-haired lunatics will roam the dripping peninsulas. Moisture will gleam on the beak of the Raven. Ancient shamans, rained from their rest in dead tree trunks, will clack their clamshell teeth in the submerged doorways of video parlors. Rivers will swell, sloughs will ferment. Vapors will billow from the troll-infested ditches, challenging windshield wipers, disguising telephone booths. Water will stream off eaves and umbrellas. It will take on the colors of the beer signs and headlamps. It will glisten on the claws of nighttime animals.

And it will rain a screaming. And it will rain a rawness. And it will rain a disorder, and hair-raising hisses from the oldest snake in the world.

Rain will hiss on the freeways. It will hiss around the prows of fishing boats. It will hiss in electrical substations, on the tips of lit cigarettes, and in the trash fires of the dispossessed. Legends will wash from the desecrated burial grounds, graffiti will run down alley walls. Rain will eat the old warpaths, spill the huckleberries, cause toadstools to rise like loaves. It will make poets drunk and winos sober, and polish the horns of the slugs.

And it will rain a miracle. And it will rain a comfort. And it will rain a sense of salvation from the philistinic graspings of the world.

Yes, I'm here for the weather. And when I'm lowered at last into a pit of marvelous mud, a pillow of fern and skunk cabbage beneath my skull, I want my epitaph to read, IT RAINED ON HIS PARADE. AND HE WAS GLAD!

TOM ROBBINS, who has made his home in La Conner, Washington, since April Fools' Day, 1970, displays the irreverent wit of the school smart aleck. But all that party-boyishness belies a serious, methodical writer whose deep, abiding interest is in accurately representing anti-establishment life through his art of writing.

◇

Robbins was born in Appalachia, in North Carolina hillbilly country, where his father worked for the Public Utility District. He attended schools in North Carolina and Virginia and began writing at age five. "My themes were outrageous, often making fun of teachers. After a while, most teachers said 'Stop writing, please,'" he says with a half-hidden smile. "When I was fifteen I wrote a review of the movie *The Outlaw* [featuring the voluptuous Jane Russell]. In those small towns in the rural South, the movie was scandalous. Blushing like a strawberry, the teacher read the review in class. She was enjoying it but couldn't admit it."

All the while, Robbins's parents were encouraging him to read and write. His mother had a love of books, and his father also was a great reader. His mother even offered to send him to creative writing classes. "I played basketball and was a jock in high school—I even went to military

school for a year in Virginia," Robbins remembers, "but I was a secret reader and clandestine intellectual."

He went on to college at Washington and Lee University, and while writing sports for the school newspaper, he worked for the acclaimed writer Tom Wolfe, "the literary star on campus."

◇

Robbins left college after he was kicked out of his fraternity for participating in a food fight. He hit the road and hitchhiked through the South, stopping along the way to do construction work . He ended his trip in Greenwich Village, wondering what to do. The answer came to him in the form of a draft notice.

He spent three years in the air force, stationed in South Korea and commuting between Korea and Japan. "I taught meteorology to the South Korean air force, although I didn't see why they needed it—they flew right through the storms," he remembers. While running a black-market ring in cigarettes and toilet articles on the side, Robbins worked for the military four days on and four days off. On his days off he hitched a plane ride to Japan, each week for a year, to visit a Japanese girlfriend. He also began to study Japanese aesthetics in Tokyo with an East Indian scholar and became especially interested in the visual arts there.

Following his stint in the air force, Robbins went back to Richmond and entered Virginia Commonwealth University, studying the history and theory of art, drama, and music, earning a bachelor's degree in aesthetics. At the same time, he wrote for the leading Virginia newspaper, the *Richmond Times-Dispatch*, and continued to work as a copyeditor after graduating with honors.

◇

Six or seven months later, he "hopped into a Plymouth Valiant and set out for Seattle, the furthest place from Richmond I could get. I had studied about Mark Tobey and Morris Graves. I was curious about the Northwest Mystic Painters. It was Seattle during the World's Fair—I thought I could get a job for sure. I drove out in the middle of winter by the shortest route, through North Dakota and Minnesota," he reminisces, adding that the car's vent broke and the snow came in. "I was on the last leg of Interstate 90, and when I rolled across the floating bridge and through the tunnel, Seattle looked so good to me."

Robbins drove up Boren Avenue and saw a FOR RENT sign. Of his last hundred dollars, he spent eighty-five for his first month's rent and ten for groceries and Olympia beer. By the next week he had been hired at *The Seattle Times* to fill in for a features editor leaving on sabbatical.

He began by editing *Dear Abby, Ask Andy,* and the garden pages. For two quarters he was also in graduate school in Far East studies. Then he was hired as features editor Lou Guzzo's assistant and art critic. In a couple of months Guzzo developed health problems, and Robbins took over, reviewing everything from symphony concerts to museum exhibits. He wrote quirky, untraditional reviews, and he remembers with pride when Seattle Symphony conductor Milton Katims invited him over to explain his review linking actor Robert Mitchum with the composer Gioacchino Rossini. When Guzzo returned to work, Robbins continued as the *Times'* visual art critic for another two and a half years.

◇

In 1964, Robbins took off for New York to research a book about master painter Jackson Pollock, who had just died. "That's what I said I was going to do, but actually I wanted to find someone besides me who had taken LSD," he admits. "I suspected there must be a psychedelic scene in New York. I should have gone to San Francisco." But he did research the book, meeting abstract expressionist painters and talking at length with such artists as Barnett Newman and Tony Smith. Finally he decided that he wanted to make his own art, rather than write about art created by others.

Returning to Seattle after two years, he found the beginnings of a countercultural scene that interested him greatly. To continue his research on this phenomenon, he talked the managing editor at the *Seattle Post-Intelligencer* into sending him to San Francisco to cover the first-ever LSD conference. "The Avalon Ballroom was filled with costumes, and the Grateful Dead, Janis Joplin, and Captain Beefheart were on stage."

By 1967, with a growing psychedelic community in Seattle, Robbins began to chronicle this revolutionary anti-establishment happening and its characters. "I wanted to portray those times, describe it from the inside out," he says. "I began by writing vignettes to amuse my girlfriend." These vignettes would become the groundwork of the first of many novels, *Another Roadside Attraction* (1971). It was based on the prototype of a young female, "a new hippie chick, the nature sprite, a celebratory figure, gotten up in gypsy clothes and spangles." His writing tried to recreate and evoke the true mood of the sixties, but instead of mere reportage, he wanted to base the book on a psychedelic model in both style and content. *Rolling Stone* called *Another Roadside Attraction* the quintessential sixties novel.

Robbins was now writing for *Seattle Magazine* while at the same time creating "happenings," or performance art events, as they are now called, and curating shows of visual art. A column he wrote about this life made its way to a book editor. "We were living in Ballard above a machine shop when I got the letter from the Doubleday editor. He came to Seattle, we met, and he encouraged me to finish the book."

Robbins moved to South Bend, on Willapa Bay in southwest Washington, where he found a storefront to rent for eight dollars a month. His girlfriend had a job at a restaurant, so they ate leftovers. On weekends he commuted to Seattle to work on the copy desk at the *Post-Intelligencer*. After the success of *Another Roadside Attraction*, he received an advance of five thousand dollars for another book and moved to La Conner.

He chose La Conner initially for its role in the history of art in the Northwest (it was home to many painters of the Northwest School), but also because Betty Bowen, public relations maven at the Seattle Art Museum, had lived there and had introduced him to people who supported his work.

◇

In subsequent years, Robbins produced six books, which sold more than five million copies and have been translated into eleven languages. For a while, he commuted between a country home in Burlington and a condominium in Seattle's Pike Place Market. Recently, though, he moved back to La Conner. "Things are different in the Skagit Valley now," he admits. "There is better food and better movies."

In recent years, the completion of each book has been followed by an extended trip. Robbins has visited Africa three times for adventure trips, usually with European stops on the way back. He's gone on a study trip with Joseph Campbell, has rafted in Sumatra and Tanzania, and has hiked the African savannah. In Timbuktu, in Mali on the Sahara, he contracted a virus that debilitated him for ten months.

His next trip is expected to take him to the Buddhist kingdom of Bhutan. Robbins himself is not actively religious, but claims linkages with spiritual teachings. He is a self-proclaimed "active foe of organized religions because they are dangerously reactionary and not at all spiritual. I practice my own blend of pantheism with Zen, Taoist, Tantric, Sufi, and Gnostic strains."

◇

For all his traveling, Robbins is a family man and was close to his parents, both of whom have died. "I would have liked to live nearer to them, but I did

go to visit more in recent years. My mother was delighted I was a writer. My father, who had wanted me to become a pharmacist, was proud of my success, although the books were too racy for him and the relatives to read. They just read the reviews."

◊

Robbins's life in the Northwest revolves around his contacts in the arts. However, he doesn't write art criticism anymore, finding that "it's a kind of writing that doesn't really serve the world. I enjoy art too much to write about it. I don't know many writers—most of my friends are painters."

Robbins is now finishing a twelve-part book, "about life, death, and goofiness," as well as "finances, the economy, frogs, and extraterrestrials."

Beluga Baby: An Afterlife of Animals

Brenda Peterson

A man bends over to embrace the gleaming gray newborn beluga; his mouth presses against its tiny, unbreathing blowhole. The calf's small black eyes still move on each side of its domed head as it struggles for air. Gasping, the biologist breathes life into this small whale, cradling it in his arms as all around the zoo staff shouts, "Breathe, breathe!"

But the baby beluga is still, eyes fixed wide open. It never takes a breath; it dies in the man's arms. These biologists at the Point Defiance Zoo in Tacoma, Washington, have to make a terrible decision: should they allow the mother beluga to keep her dead calf as in the wild, or should the staff whisk the newborn away for a necropsy to determine the cause of death? Science at last wins out and the staff moves the calf from the cold, bloody pool, leaving Mauyak, the mother beluga, to thrash about in confusion and pain. Another staff member, Alan, stays with Mauyak for three hours after the birth.

◆

"She kept rolling over the scuba divers in a slow-motion embrace, trying to understand," he told me when I visited the zoo after the sorrowful birth. "This was, after all, Mauyak's first delivery," he explained. "And I don't know if she even realized her calf was dead before they took him away. The two whales, Mauyak and the young female Shikku, were in the pool. Neither beluga had ever experienced birth, but we hoped Shikku would act as a midwife the way whales in the wild do for each other: the midwife whale will lift the newborn to the surface for its first breath. But it turns out Shikku didn't have to swim the calf to the surface, because after a very difficult labor—Mauyak corkscrewing and twisting in the small pool for hours—the little calf struggled out, flukes first, and floated himself to the surface.

"Everyone started cheering and clapping, because they believed the baby took a breath. But the calf just floated up there too quietly, then started sinking. Shikku and Mauyak lifted the little calf back up to the surface, and I yelled to another researcher to grab the calf and pull him up to the float to see if he was breathing. That's when we realized the calf had never taken his first breath. Our artificial respiration was hopeless because, as we later found out from the necropsy, his blowhole valve was disengaged, broken somehow . . . perhaps in all the labor. But we don't really know why. Belugas—especially their first birthing—are such a mystery. Fifty percent of firstborns die, even in the wild."

♦

I was walking with Alan and my friend Flor, a photographer, down to
the zoo's Rocky Shores exhibit, home to three beluga whales: Mauyak,
Shikku, and a male named Inuk. We walked slowly as Alan told his
story. Outside the entrance to the big chilly pool with its glass underwater wall—through which zoogoers can be eye-to-eye with a great
beluga—Alan hesitated. "I haven't been back here since the birth, I
mean the death," he said softly, his brown eyes pensive. "Mauyak may
still be angry with me—with all of us."

"Did Mauyak ever get a chance to say good-bye to her calf?"

Alan lowered his voice. "No," he said.

As we approached the pool, Shikku and Inuk greeted Alan, whom
they've known for over four years, with the chirps and whistles that
earn this white whale the name "sea canary." But Mauyak swam immediately away to the back pool, a red rubber buoy balanced on her huge,
pale forehead. "A whale will carry her dead newborn like that until it
disintegrates," Alan said. "In the wild, if a mother whale can't hold on
to the real newborn's body, she will find a net, plank, even a caribou
carcass to carry as her lost surrogate calf."

As Mauyak swam slowly in circles, careful to keep the buoy-baby
on the surface, as if to let it breathe, even the children watching understood this ritual of grief. "That's her pretend baby," a young boy explained to his sister, without having to be told. The small crowd was
quiet, all eyes on Mauyak as she floated, making no contact with her
mate, her female companion Shikku, her friend Alan, or the crowd.
"For almost a week after the delivery, she wouldn't look us in the eye,"
Alan murmured. "She's usually so gregarious."

♦

I well remembered Mauyak's playful intimacies. In the spring of 1989,
the first time I met Mauyak and the other whales, I'd been startled by
their openness. They spurted me with water, opening vast mouths to
take my hand against their tongues (their way of touching me), and
allowed me to feed and stroke them. I was so happy to make contact
with these whales closer to home, after half a decade of swimming with
dolphins far off in the Florida Keys. Also on that spring day I was fortunate enough to meet a tiny harbor porpoise named Magic who'd been
found motherless, stranded on a Washington coast shore. This fine fellow, only the length of my arm, so trusted Alan that he allowed Alan to
lift him briefly before splashing back into the pool. The next time I met
Magic, a year later, he'd grown into a zoo favorite for his high-spirited
antics. He was often let into the big pool with the three belugas, where

he'd flirt shamelessly with them, sometimes being mistaken by the crowds for a little gray beluga baby.

The last time I'd seen Magic was in July 1992, when Mauyak was thirteen months pregnant, due in August. In stately maternity, Mauyak had kept her distance from the others, a lady in waiting. But Magic darted in between Shikku and Inuk. Stroking Shikku's white belly with his snout, snapping at Inuk over a float toy, Magic was all mischief. In a twirling ballet, he shot straight out of the water, dove deep, then nipped at Shikku's open mouth in a series of small kisses. From all this silly courtship, Mauyak held herself aloof, seeking solitude in the back pool. Did she anticipate then that she would deliver a calf destined to live only minutes?

◆

"We know so damn little about belugas . . . especially their birthing," Alan said, stepping back from the pool to allow Mauyak her privacy. "Of the eight belugas born in captivity, only two have survived." He led us to the back of the pool for a closer look. Even after twenty years of researching and working with dolphins and other whales, Alan believes we know only a quarter of what we should about cetaceans. "The limits, you know, are not in the whales," he said. "They are in us."

He told of an experiment he had conducted with dolphins in which he placed eye cups on them and asked the dolphins to recognize certain symbols with their echolocation. "It took me months to design that experiment," Alan said, laughing. "And those dolphins learned the symbols in five minutes. So I had to devise a more difficult problem. But they kept figuring it all out until I no longer had the technology to test their abilities. The last test I could design was discerning a symbol through sonar that was only one-thousandth of an inch square. They aced that! While they were at it, they also identified different carbon densities in metal rods, and differentiated colors."

Alan shook his head and led us into an enclosure with a giant plastic swimming pool. Inside raced a tiny dark porpoise, his dorsal fin no bigger than my three fingers. It was yet another stranded newborn, only several weeks old. The little one zoomed around the pool at the sight of Alan, his exhalation a tiny *twoosh* of moist air that delicately tickled my palms raised about a foot above the surface of the water.

Alan smiled wistfully and greeted the baby porpoise by making a series of sucking clicks and whistles. Delightedly the porpoise spun around, then dove and swam speed circles before surfacing for another stroke. The staff was hand-feeding him every two hours. They had not yet named the harbor porpoise in case he did not survive—as if this might protect them from his painful loss.

"We lost Magic, you know," Alan said under his breath, as if to protect the small porpoise, with its cetacean super-ultrasonic hearing, from his words. "I know," I said, remembering my first post-delivery visit to Mauyak, when I'd been shocked to hear that Magic had died only days after I'd last seen him flirting with Shikku, several weeks before Mauyak's delivery. That bright summer day Magic had simply sunk to the bottom of the pool, having succumbed to the cetacean's most dreaded death: drowning. Cetaceans will beach themselves rather than drown. The necropsy did not reveal any cause of death. Here was another mystery to add to the inscrutable beluga birthing process.

The Point Defiance Zoo staff was still desolate after the loss of Magic and of Mauyak's calf in less than two months. It showed in the tender concern and tentative hope for this new porpoise's survival. As one of the women staff members said, "We're all grief-stricken. We did everything we could—the best technology in the country, the constant monitoring of everything from blood to water quality. But it was no good." She paused and sighed, sadly, "It makes you wonder, doesn't it? It's too bad there isn't heaven for animals."

♦

Her words disturbed me deeply. Why is it, I wondered, that our Western idea of heaven is a world in which everyone but us is extinct? Are we here below as above, unconsciously enacting a mythical heaven-on-earth as we watch species after species die out? How did we get so separated from our animals that our religion imagines heaven to be a place where we live forever without animal companionship?

The older myths—Native American, pagan, and even Old Testament—are inexorably linked to animals. Often Native American tribes divided their members into animal clans. The pagans revered animals; ancient Greeks listened to their Delphic oracle python. The Old Testament God instructed Noah to build an ark to weather the destruction of the world by water. Back then, God included animals in this floating afterlife. But now we've dwindled down to our modern-day mainstream religion's concept of heaven for humans alone. How clearly this mythology betrays our isolation and loneliness here on Earth.

♦

As I stood with the others at the Point Defiance poolside, watching the tiny surviving porpoise spin and twirl beneath our outstretched hands, I felt my sadness lift. "He's so alive," I marveled. "He's *got* to make it."

"Some of the staff secretly call him 'The Kid,'" Alan said, smiling. "They believe if we name him, he'll stay with us. I mean, after all, it is quite a coincidence that this little calf was stranded only days before Mauyak's calf died. Some of us wanted to let this porpoise into the pool with Mauyak to adopt as her baby. But the vote went against it."

My hands were numb now from the cold water of the baby harbor porpoise tank. As I gently slapped the water's surface, the calf lifted his glossy short black snout and shot between my palms. At that moment my friend Flor laughed out loud and started taking pictures. I looked over at her standing by the beluga pool and saw her splashed from waist to feet. "Mauyak did it," Flor said happily. "Go for it," Alan said under his breath. "Mauyak's calling to you. Maybe she can play more with strangers right now than with the staff."

We left the harbor porpoise tank and leaned over the deep back pool, where both Mauyak and Inuk were splurting water at our feet. Inside Inuk's wide-open mouth lay several fish, as if he were offering to share his supper with us. I was accustomed to Inuk's playfulness, but the astonishing change was in Mauyak. For the moment she seemed relieved of her mourning, just as she had left the red buoy-baby on the other side of the pool.

Here now she raised herself up by her pectoral fins and came halfway out of the water to lift my hand with her huge forehead. The action reminded me of my cat when he wants affection. Happily I gave it, overjoyed to see Mauyak's openness. She slid gracefully under my outstretched hand in a leisurely manner. My open palm tingled with the cool, fast elegance of whale skin, like a scarf of wet, raw silk being pulled sensually through my fingers.

◆

Whale skin is a marvel of sensitivity and skills—twenty times more sensitive than a human's. But cetacean sensitivity does not stop at the skin. Whales use echoes in their sonar to hear one another's bodies and therefore read each other's emotional and physical states. Humans have finally caught up with cetaceans in the much more limited technology of ultrasound. But what we cannot duplicate is the extreme sophistication of whale echolocation. Echolocation is three-dimensional: its vibrations can bounce off the inside cavities of the body, listening and gauging the echoes sounding from the brain, the heart, the kidneys, liver, even the ovaries. It is common among those who swim with dolphins to find them herding a pregnant woman away from the other swimmers, encircling her as dolphin midwives. Many women have first discovered they were pregnant while swimming with dolphins, before they or ultrasound could confirm it.

Recently, human technology has come up with our own sophisticated sonar. According to Alan Sutphen, a medical doctor who is also involved with cetaceans, from our own Doppler ultrasound-test echoes we can hear "the flow of blood through the microscopic capillaries of the finger . . . as a veritable roar." Sutphen goes on to say, in an essay in Joan McIntyre's collection *Mind in the Waters*, that "cetaceans are aware of each other's health and general well-being. Cancers and tumors must be self-evident. Strokes and heart attacks are as obvious as moles on our skins." Along with scanning the physiological state, cetaceans have the ability to recognize emotional fluctuations such as "sexual arousal, fear, depression, and excitement."

In other words, there is no hiding place from such sophisticated scanning. What would life be for humans if we lived in a world without clothes or skin to stop our sensing skills? We might all become psychics, able to clearly see one another's deepest emotions and inner body. The world of appearances would be replaced by an inner knowledge we can barely fathom, for it would be both sensory and emotional.

Skin that echoes, skin that dreams—this is the whale skin. This is the whale skin I stroked in my first meeting with the great belugas. This is the astonishingly cool and elastic whale skin my hands have memorized. One of my nephews, whom I took swimming with the dolphins, once cried out, "She feels like cold honeydew melon!" That is the touch, but the elegant buoyancy, the movement under the hand is harder to explain. When I stroked Mauyak's forehead, that huge oil-filled melon used for echolocation, its gleaming expanse throbbed and pulsed under my palm like a gigantic heart. I could watch that white dome expand and retreat like a wave atop her head. "Otherworldly" is the only way I can describe this sensation—like meeting an alien mind that moves alongside mine, but so unfathomably. I can only rest my hand on such a mind as it works, scans and records and responds. All I know is that the feeling is utterly distinct, a blissful communion.

Perhaps it is true, as some researchers believe, that belugas and other cetaceans exist in an alpha state their entire lives. We do know that their brains never really sleep or slip into unconsciousness as do humans'. But cetaceans must mindfully take each breath; if a whale loses consciousness it will drown. Only one hemisphere of a cetacean brain rests at a time. In the wild, scientists have observed pods of dolphins in which all those on one side swim with one eye closed; those swimming guard on the other side of the pod will have the opposite eye closed. So even as they rest one side of their brain, they are aware.

Continual consciousness, an environment that floats their bodies just as water floats our human brains, and a mind that never shuts down. What are they thinking all those hours in the ocean? How differently does their intelligence develop without using so much of their brains to operate hands as we do? Why do cetacean species rarely kill their own kind or, except for the orca when very hungry, devour their own kin? Do these big-brained mammals have something to teach us about survival, about altruism and consciousness?

◆

These are questions I mused over as Mauyak opened her gigantic mouth to take my small hand, her pink tongue as soft as a baby's face against my palm. Her forehead throbbed, her great black eye opened wide as if to take me in, body and soul. My hand felt the rows of tiny round teeth tender against my skin. She held my hand, but she sounded all of me. And I trusted her with all my heart. With one flick of her mighty flukes this beluga could have bitten into my hand and dragged me underwater, her massive thousand-pound bulk easily drowning me. But never has a beluga harmed a human. They treat us with the mothering kindness of a gentle giant toward a smaller species still struggling to understand.

As Mauyak held my hand in her mouth I wondered, Are whales somehow carrying our species in this world—the way whales will mournfully carry a calf or lift a newborn up to the surface for air? Are whales waiting with their cetacean consciousness for us to wake up from our long slumber, the dream in which we believe we are alone here, that we are the only minds at work on this planet? Do whales wait for us to discover the humility within ourselves to recognize our mammal kinship and then take the next baby step: apprentice ourselves to another species' way of being at one with the world?

◆

Here in the Northwest, this apprenticeship is still possible. The Northwest Native American tribes teach us that the original People of Puget Sound were the animals—salmon, whale, raven, eagle, and wolf, among others. These animals still live alongside us, not only in myth but in our natural, daily lives. According to local tribal legends, these animals can go between the worlds, metamorphosing into their human kin and back again. It is said, for example, that Orca and Salmon People return in their mighty migrations to confirm the survival of all species. What would we do if the Salmon and Whale People didn't return one year? Our human tribe would be lost, too.

Living along this Northwest coast, one cannot help but feel a part of the animals' natural cycles—whether it's the salmon's spawning return or the gray whales' astonishing journey from the Arctic feeding grounds to Baja, Mexico, birthing lagoons. In the far north, belugas still swim in pale families against glowing glaciers.

In the San Juan Islands, resident pods of orcas come so near Lime Kiln Point, off Friday Harbor, that the rocks can be scratching posts to scrape barnacles off their luminous bellies. The Friday Harbor Whale Museum has been tracking these orcas for decades and can identify and study their pod families in the wild. Whale watching of both the resident orcas and the migrating gray whales is a Northwest initiation into the mysteries of the water world alongside our own land life.

But do we who live here by water have the humility to learn from our mammalian kin? After over a decade in the Northwest, I cannot imagine not living on Puget Sound. She is my teacher more deeply than any Zen master or guru; her tides and lessons remind me daily that I am part of something far greater than myself. And to her creatures—from the Salmon to the Whale People—I have apprenticed my mind and my work. Surely I will learn balance and wisdom from the whales, if I can keep my heart open to their voices. If the humpbacks off Hawaii can sing and pass on lullabies to their young, orcas and grays and Dall's porpoises can school me in intimacy and community. The belugas, those captive white whales I visit like nearby relatives, have already taught me much about loss and grieving.

◆

We are at a crisis in our environmental relationships that begs for new models of thinking about ourselves and the world. We've been the "master race" for so long that our relationship with the planet and its animals is like that of totalitarian dictators and their subjects. But with totalitarianism falling in some parts of the world, it's time for the Berlin Wall between our species and others to fall, too.

Centuries ago we believed the entire universe revolved around our planet. Since then, we've figured out that ours is one of many planets that orbit the sun. It always takes our minds a while to catch up with scientific revelations. Modern-day psychics are telling us that if you look at something, you change it. How might simply looking at other species as equals change our future, our chances for survival? The Bible predicts that "the meek shall inherit the earth." I'd expand "the meek" to include cockroaches and pioneer rats and crocodiles—

all veteran survivors, heirs to this lush planet. Is it possible for us to imagine a world that might one day simply select *against* our species in order to survive? The ancient concept of Gaia, the Earth Mother, has been revised in some scientific circles to declare that Earth is a living, sentient organism ever balancing and maintaining herself. Another current theory is the "New Story," which recounts the drama of this planet with Earth as the major character and humans as minor players. We may well strut and fret our small lives for not too many more generations.

Our fate as a species has always depended upon our ability to adapt and change in response to environmental exigencies. Only in the most recent centuries of reason and technology did we presume to separate our fate from that of nature and other species. But Earth is changing and it is our fate to adapt to this planet, not vice versa. Our religions must now remember this truth and celebrate again our dependence upon nature, our interdependence with all living creatures. If we can restore our perspective, we may well survive.

When we bring our hearts, minds, and myths into an open relationship with the natural world, we cease to be deadweight that the world must carry. How long will nature carry us? Will Earth, like those great whales, carry us until we disintegrate? Is Earth, like that beluga mother, in mourning, grieving over the human part of herself that has died?

◆

As my hand lay palm-open in Mauyak's huge mouth, I felt she held the whole of me—deeply, tenderly. Her eyes also held me: unblinking, utterly aware. I felt a great wave of grief wash over me, tears blurring my eyes. My heart opened and I felt the calm and clear stillness between us. "I know . . . " I said softly, "I know." Mauyak gently eased her mouth open and let my hand float in the water near her jaw. She turned on her side, without breaking our gaze. Then she slipped her huge head beneath my hand and I stroked her from melon to flukes. In slow elegy, the beluga swam across the pool to retrieve her floating buoy—the baby that will never disintegrate, the calf that could not stay in this world.

Let us stay in the world, I wanted to say to Mauyak. *Let my species and yours stay together, kin here on this blue, sea-encircled planet.*

Mauyak brought her buoy-baby back to me and drifted just out of arm's reach, again holding my eye with hers. We held that gaze for so long it seemed that together we held the whole world between us, as if our gaze was a gravity that kept the world spinning. And who knows what other worlds besides?

Looking at Mauyak, then as now, I believe that the beluga baby is as much alive in spirit as my own beloved grandfather, as alive as any of my species gone to another world. And when I join those of my human and animal family gone before me, I expect my afterlife to be surrounded by all species—from the serpents to the eagles, from the jaguars to the cockroaches. And in that afterlife of animals, that spirit-ark that carries us all alike, I'll look to swim alongside a gleaming bright beluga baby.

BRENDA PETERSON, a prolific writer with several books of fiction and essays to her credit, is deeply committed to addressing the connections between humans and the natural world, and the destruction of that natural world. She feels a closeness to and an ability to communicate with animals, and believes that humans have much to learn from the animal kingdom.

◊

Peterson was born in Quincy, California, about 100 miles south of the Oregon border, and lived her early years on several million acres of national forest—her father worked for the United States Forest Service.

"There was no clearcutting then," she says, "and the first two sounds I heard were wind through the trees, the pine and blue spruce, and my mother's typing. She was writing a book about the railroading days on the Wabash. In four and a half years, we rarely left the forest lookout station where we lived with several other families. My only playmates were forest animals—my first two years I rarely saw other human children. I crawled on the forest floor, memorizing it with my hands. Nature was like Braille for me.

"My first memory was lying on a rock, and being awakened as a huge rattlesnake loomed in my face with its tongue sticking out. It was a sunny day—I had no fear. But my father came along and killed it immediately. He cut off the rattle for me as a toy. I was horrified and upset; I cried for a long time because a holy communion had been disrupted."

Feeling the snake is still important to her, Peterson has adopted it as a totem. "I always felt hardly human. As a seven-year-old, I wrote an essay on the mistreatment of horses. I was obsessed with not only loving horses, but *being* a horse. I think I bonded first with animals."

Eventually the family left the forest in California. They moved every eighteen months to different parts of the country, as Peterson's father worked his way up to the office of chief of the Forest Service. Peterson remembers, "We often didn't even unpack. We couldn't have many possessions. In fact, I have no possessions left from my childhood. We had to hustle to keep up academically. We constantly were thrown into situations where we had to be quick studies. My sister says we were moving so much it was like dropping acid but never coming back."

Peterson always wrote to keep track of the changing landscape around her—not diaries, but massive dream journals. "The only center was in my relations with my siblings, and my bond with the natural territory. I tried to write about the places we left. I was aware of the fragility of our future, because we never went back.

"Every summer we went to visit our grandparents; that was our only constancy," she adds. "My father's family lived in the Ozarks—they were proud white trash. We lived there the longest time for us—five years—in the Deep South.

"It was a period when people were shocked by the Kennedy and Dr. King murders. I don't think people

out West ever really understood that time," Peterson says. "I went to Kennedy's funeral—it was in the midst of the integration of the South, a very violent time. Everyone was obsessed with nukes and the missile crisis. I felt we were living day to day.

"We lived with duck-and-cover drills. Everyone had fallout shelters. I and my brother and two sisters made our own contingency plan to escape with our favorite ichthyosaurus [a dinosaur precursor of the dolphins]. He would carry us to safety because we knew this world would be destroyed and fallout shelters couldn't save us. It would be a rescue to another dimension. I felt that my real mother—my earth—would be destroyed. Even as a child in 1962, it was clear to me that with nuclear bombs they could literally destroy the earth."

◊

After graduation from the University of California at Davis, and a short, miserable stay in Georgia, Peterson went to New York and worked for *The New Yorker* for five years. "I was an editorial assistant, another name for a slave. At the end, they all thought I was a failure for wanting to leave." She finally left New York for Colorado, to work a farm her family had inherited. She also was halfway through her first novel, *River of Light*, a story of the Deep South.

"I grew corn to make money and worked as a typesetter in a newspaper factory at night, doing *Rodeo Sports News* and *Cattleman's Gazette*, really blue-collar work." Peterson also worked as fiction editor for *Rocky Mountain Magazine*. Knopf published *River of Light* in 1978, when she was twenty-eight years old. She was asked to teach at the University of Arizona and began commuting because she didn't want to give up living in the Colorado mountains.

During this time she came to visit a friend who lived in Seattle, and fell in love with Puget Sound in the middle of winter. "I immediately saw that living by water was a sanctuary and companion to the mystical," she says. "It is an ambiguous, androgynous world where everything is violet and gray, a visual atmosphere where you can't tell what time it is sometimes. The horizons and boundaries blur. I decided I must stay on Puget Sound, living on the water, and that means I'll probably be a renter all my life to afford it." Peterson has been living in the Northwest for twelve years, a radical act for her or any member of her transient family. "Everyone else in the family keeps moving; I'm the only one staying put here in the West. I've decided it's an important thing for me to commit, because the next generation needs these roots.

"I will not be moved from this body of water. She is my mentor and the only guru I will ever follow," she says. "If I can memorize this land and bond with Puget Sound, I can heal this long-haunted time of everything shifting."

Peterson was first employed in Seattle as a typesetter for *The Rocket* and *Seattle Weekly* ("I can type like a demon"), doing freelance editing on the side. She then worked at REI (Recreational Equipment, Inc.) for seven years. "I was a typesetter there, then taught writing to the staff, then became an environmental writer, which coincided with my father becoming chief of the Forest Service," she says.

"I somehow had to counteract him—I carry things for him, I carry his Native American side, which he didn't claim. So I carried the forest, while he rose to power in the bureaucracy of the Forest Service, at first during the Carter administration, then under Reagan and Watt," she says. "There was trouble with the old-growth forests; he was constantly in the fray. He actually did fight for old forests, but to little avail. There was weariness in that. When he finally left government, I felt I was freed from my job after those years in corporate communications."

Since then, Peterson has been writing books and teaching private writing students, finding a kinship and depth with the community that she feels one doesn't get teaching in a university. She is now working on a book called *Sister Stories*, about her life and relationships with her two sisters.

Aside from her three published novels, *River of Light, Becoming the Enemy*, and *Duck and Cover*, Peterson is a widely published nature writer, with two essay collections, *Living by Water: True Stories of Nature and Spirit* and *Nature and Other Mothers*. Selections from *Living by Water* have been widely anthologized, especially the chapter titled "Animals as Brothers and Sisters," about Peterson's swims with dolphins.

She is interested in bringing people back together with the natural world through narratives. Moreover, she feels compelled to get bureaucratic land managers together with poets, storytellers, and Native elders in every type of forum. "We need to bring back the ancient connection between the artists and the stewards of the land," Peterson affirms. "They have forgotten; so my job is to remind them of the true connection, which is not a scientific one, but a soul connection."

Another Life

Sam Hamill

For the past twenty minutes, a gnarly old gray rabbit has sniffed around my new moss garden. He doesn't see me watching from the window of my new studio. He sniffs the wilting stalks of lilies, then noses about the freshly washed and carefully placed river stones. He scoots up onto a cedar nurse log and inches along, sniffing as he goes.

In this morning's *Port Townsend Leader*, reviewing a fifteen-year retrospective of local artist Ed Cain's paintings, drawings, and monotypes, a writer said, "Birds, more than any other animal, mirror man's [sic] soul." What I have most admired about Ed Cain's paintings of birds all these years is precisely that they do *not* reflect a human soul (other than that of the artist, by implication); rather, what they address is a quality I would describe as the essential thusness of birdness. Birds do not exist as mere metaphor, but as bird consciousness achieving a form. Cain articulates what could be called an essence of birdness in his abstract images.

One might be tempted to paraphrase a famous Zen *koan* (question): "Does that rabbit exist outside your mind or inside your mind?" To which I can only reply, "Yes."

This past summer, my nineteenth here, I designed and had built my dream studio, Kage-an, a hundred or so feet from my house, just beyond a row of tall cedars. Kage-an (a Japanese term pronounced *kah-gay-ahn* with no stressed syllable): *Kage* means shadow; *an* indicates the "ten-foot-square hut" of a retired Zen monk but by the time of Basho (seventeenth century) included the hermitage of Zen poets. Hence, "Basho-an" or "Banana-tree hermitage," from which name the poet took his final *nom de plume* of Basho.

My retreat has a small room with standing library stacks for several thousand books, a small painting studio, a comfortable writing studio, and a storage room. Between the writing studio and the library, there is an elegant *shoji* (paper and wood) door made by a local craftsman. Another woodworker made my oak desk. Kage-an, my shadow retreat.

Now I watch the old rabbit disappear into the undergrowth. He may be gone from the garden, but he remains, for the moment, in mind. Just as this building, before I cut down the first tree, rose first in mind. But before the many years of living here, of clearing land and building my house by hand, of noting the names of things and the cycles of seasons, it was vague, ill-defined. It did not rise by chance, and certainly not without daily practice. Kage-an evolved as my knowledge of local wisdom grew. In what direction does groundwater drain? What is the angle of sunlight in any particular season? My hermitage is a physical expression of my own sense of the Buddhist concept of right mindfulness.

♦

I've read many talks on what is meant by "right mindfulness" as it is used in the "eightfold path" to enlightenment in the *Lotus Sutra*. As a lay Buddhist, I read it first in a very literal way: mindful as "mind full," as a filled hand becomes a handful—with both "positive" and "negative" implications. But simultaneously, the term suggests being filled with care. I don't know the Sanskrit term which the Indian scholar Kumarajiva translated into the fourth-century Chinese that scholars now use as the most reliable text. But even the Sanskrit was a translation from some unknown Central Asian tongue. It is a fittingly stimulating text for interpenetrating minds that span centuries. This is text that has given definition to my practice, both as writer and as "Zenist" (student of Zen).

Last summer, deer ate my roses and stripped my plum trees. To-day, I murdered a gopher in my lawn. Does the practice of right mindfulness include the execution of a gopher while excluding the execution of deer? Or do I, as one friend suggested, "give back the lawn to nature"? Which sounds fine. Except that the lawn was never made of anything other than nature in the first place. The house is nature. Sariputra, wisest disciple of Buddha, was admonished by another disciple, Vimalakirti, "You must achieve liberation without avoiding the passions that rule the world."

Having a place in this world has been a hunger and a passion all my days, a hunger that comes naturally to an orphan. Achieving "highest perfect enlightenment" has not. So much for transcending desire, that root of all suffering.

That dirty gull with its astonishing cry expresses only birdness, only gullness. In one of his most famous poems, "Night Thoughts While Traveling," the T'ang dynasty poet Tu Fu laments his aloneness and concludes, "Adrift, drifting, what is left for the lone gull / adrift between earth and heaven?" Rather than seeking human qualities in the bird, he searches for a sense of gullness within himself. He does this time and again in his poems—with the wild goose, with crows. The quality of his mindfulness is almost the opposite of that of the poets who dominate Western culture, and certainly runs contrary to the mind-set of our local art critic in the *Port Townsend Leader*.

Like the bear and the cougar, I have sought a niche. Like a dog, I have left my mark. Like the water, I have tried to remain level, but have often fallen hard. And now I have made manifest the workplace carried in my heart's mind, evolving since childhood. By American standards, it is modest. But by the standards of the classical Chinese and Japanese poets who have provided me with a model for my life, it is downright luxurious. So, like cougar, bear, or raven, there are times when I punish or kill what invades. Let the deer enjoy my plum leaves and my plums; I can screen or surrender my roses. But the gopher is dead, and for the time being, he decomposes slowly in my mind, and that's the stink of that particular deed.

To many friends, the fact of the red fox crossing my yard as she sniffs along the rabbit trail is extraordinary. Tall trees, silent nights, bamboo and moss and stone—all extraordinary. And I too am astonished to waken in my fiftieth year as to another life. And enter, perhaps, what I hope will be a long closing phase. It is all a gift.

◆

Near my desk, I've hung a long scroll. It is Tu Fu's "Heading South," one of his last poems:

> Spring returns to Peach Blossom River
> and my sail is a cloud through maple forests.
>
> Exiled, I lived for years in secret, moving on
> farther from home with tear-stains on my sleeves.
>
> Now old and sick, at last I'm headed south.
> Remembering old friends, I look back north one final time.
>
> A hundred years I sang my bitter song,
> but not a soul remembers those old rhymes.

Tu Fu, arguably China's greatest poet, had virtually no readership in his lifetime other than a handful of (mindful) "poetry friends." I spent nearly ten years going to school on Tu Fu. He's a challenge even for someone whose classical Chinese is good, and mine isn't. Some of those years, I spent long evenings with *Matthew's Chinese Dictionary* in pulsing kerosene light, huddled beside a wood stove. Tu Fu's gift to me was not only the poems themselves, but the attentive minds those poems attracted, minds that penetrated the poems, shedding light for struggling scholar-translator-poets like myself. He became a personal as well as a literary model.

Eventually, I made a little book, *Facing the Snow*, with about a hundred of Tu's poems. It was published by White Pine Press and sold out over a few years. I was paid in copies. The scroll is in Chinese, a gift from the hand of Canada's Yim Tse, one of the great calligraphers in the world and a gracious soul who also contributed several other poems in Chinese calligraphy for publication in the book. When I offered to pay for his work, he replied, "Oh no, I couldn't possibly take money for writing Tu Fu's poems."

Eventually, the publisher of White Pine Press, Dennis Maloney, showed the book to someone at Weatherhill, along with my translations of Li Po, *Banishment Immortal*. Weatherhill (with White Pine's permission) invited me to draw from both out-of-print books to make another, *Endless River: Tu Fu and Li Po, a Friendship in Poetry*. When *Endless River* was published in 1993, I sent a copy to my "poetry friend" Hayden Carruth, whose *Collected Shorter Poems* we had published at Copper Canyon Press, and for which he won the National Book Critics Circle Award. Several months later, Carruth sent me a suite of nineteen pages, "A Summer with Tu Fu," from which I quote only the opening lines of the opening poem:

> *What does it mean, master*
> *that across fifteen centuries*
> *I make my profoundest and so fatally*
>
> *inadequate obeisance to your*
> *monarchic presence in the kingdom*
> *of poetry? What does it mean*
>
> *that two old guys speak to one another*
> *from the sadnesses of exile,*
> *confronting their fear of final*
>
> *futility after years of futile awkwardness*
> *in the world of doing? We look,*
> *you and I, at the heron in the sunset.*

Near the end of that first poem, Carruth observes, "We are the same." In this, Carruth teaches the fundamental lesson of the *Lotus Sutra*: We are the same. In the sutra, Zen master Manjushri reminds the bodhisattvas that we must teach each in his or her own way, and that all ways are one way when the path leads to enlightenment. Buddha, one Zen master observed, is a shit-stick. Each of us is a Buddha. Each of us is a poet. Each of us commits a little murder now and then. Being, the Sakyamuni Buddha observed, is suffering. Or, as my long-ago friend Herman Robert E. Lee Prewitt of Kentucky used to say, "We'll never get out of this world alive."

When Tu Fu brings Hayden Carruth to gaze at the heron in the sunset, the heron may be supposed to be an actual heron. It is not merely a metaphor. The heron enters human perception, then exits, leaving behind only the memory of an image or the figure of memory. And how can the twentieth-century Carruth share a vision with an eighth-century poet whose original language is impenetrable from Carruth's perspective? How can they be said to stand together? Ezra Pound observed, "Genius is always contemporary"; they *do* stand together.

There is a kind of poem that is a gift of vision, a poem that might be said to have eyes. Such a vision transcends time. Carruth's is a poet's response to the discovery (the gift) of philosophic harmony and spiritual kinship. Poets in the United States live largely in the shadowlands of a subculture. The vast majority move within the university community, others within an alternative literary community. But virtually all of us live a kind of interior exile. Most Americans simply fail to comprehend how or why poetry matters. And so we poets tend to form, as Octavio Paz has noted, a kind of secret society. It is a society with open doors, to be sure; virtually everyone is welcome. But few choose to descend through the dark woods into Dante's inferno or to scale them, up into Blake's heaven. We who undertake such journeys tend to form a family or a clan, each with its siblings.

My adoptive parents, although they abused me, gave me the gift of poetry. The poet Kenneth Rexroth added Tu Fu to the list of those to whom I am indebted. Tu Fu (and Zen) brought me to Chinese. Some of the poems became poems in English, which I in turn gave away. Receiving my gift, Carruth makes another gift and sends it out into the world. The gift economy is a very real economy, albeit one that is wholly neglected in our corporate educational system. And it is within this economy that every poet struggles for sustenance.

◆

Ten years ago, I wrote my own obeisance to Tu Fu's presence in the kingdom of poetry:

> Tu Fu, old and ravaged by consumption,
> bent over his mulberry paper and wrote
> the characters "single" and "wild goose"
> his eyes weakened by the moonlight.
>
> Because it was October in his life,
> he refilled his cup with wine.
> His joys were neither large nor many.
> But they were precise.

Which is to say he did not ask for much, and he brought to his daily practice an attentive mind. The economy of the soul interpenetrates the gift economy when a poet translates a poet. A clear attentive mind, Gary Snyder wrote years ago in "Above Pate Valley," has no meaning—yet we are here. "Get rid of words, get rid of meaning," an ancient Chinese poet wrote, "and there is still poetry." Basho notes,

> Saigyo's tanka, Sogi's renga,
> Sesshu's sumi, Rikyu's tea—
> the spirit which moves them is one spirit.

The *Kokinshu* reminds us, "Poetry begins in the heart."

As a poet, it is my work to try to empty myself of selfishness in order to become a vessel for inspiration, a gift from which I make—implying discipline and craft—a gift, the poem, in order to give it away, in order to become empty. The process is more important than the product, which is merely another skinny volume of poetry, sheet music to the real noise the poem makes when it is fully embodied. Tu Fu's gift to a few poetry friends became a gift to scholars and poets who in turn helped make the poem a gift to me, a gift which I passed on, and which Carruth amplified once again. Across centuries and in a plenitude of languages this act of generosity has been repeated. Poetry, when it is properly given by the human heart and breath, is a gift that cannot be diminished, only misspoken.

Rainer Maria Rilke asked that the poem demand, "You must change your life." And everywhere I look, I find possibility, I find poems that have changed my life in subtle or profound ways. Ezra Pound asks a poet "to have drawn from the air a live tradition / and from a fine old eye the unconquered flame." Charles Olson wrote in Part II of "The Kingfishers,"

> I am no Greek, hath not th'advantage.
> And of course, no Roman:
> he can take no risk that matters,
> the risk of beauty least of all.
>
> But I have my kin, if for no other reason than
> (as he said, next of kin) I commit myself . . .

To which I might add:

> I am no Chinese or Japanese Buddhist.
> But I claim certain kinship.
> Given my freedom,
> I hold to defined commitment.

The idea of literary kinship and of literary community was very powerfully appealing to a fifteen-year-old street kid, an orphan stoked on heroin and looking for what beatniks called free love in the fifties. There is no free love, of course. But I found a sacred kinship with Kenneth Rexroth, the first real, living writer I came to know personally. I was strung out in San Francisco, sleeping in parked cars and turning tricks for dope. Rexroth gave me contemporary poetry, from Williams and Pound and H.D. to Bob Kaufman, Lenore Kandel, Denise Levertov, and Gary Snyder. I believe to this day that his gift saved my life.

From Williams, "American idiom" and "No ideas but in things"; from Ezra Pound, Confucius and "All wisdom is rooted in learning to call things by the right name," including "that stupid suburban prejudice" anti-Semitism, and the enormous beauty and final tragedy of his *Cantos'*

> Charity I have had sometimes,
>   I cannot make it flow thru,
> A little light, like a rushlight
>   to lead back to splendor . . .

after several hundred pages of a poem that is truly epochal; and Canto LXXXI's "What thou lovest well remains, / the rest is dross." H.D.'s neoclassicism; Snyder's *serious* joyful Buddhist discipline and "What You Should Know to Be a Poet"; Levertov's supreme candor; Kandel's liberating female sexuality, especially in *The Love Book*; Kaufman's street-smart ironic bebop. The roots of another life. The existentialism of Sam Beckett and the soul of commitment in Albert Camus, and the snake-like syntax of John Coltrane and supreme cool of Miles. It is miraculous, the thread that binds that life to this.

◆

And now I waken to this new room, this new building, late in a life that is rapidly growing old. Copper Canyon Press, built of the stuff of dreams over two decades with my former partner, Tree Swenson, has published more than 150 volumes of poetry. The gifts Tree bestowed on the work of the press and on my life over twenty years are clearly inestimable. So here, too, in this room, the spirit of all that work continues to bestow gifts with every breath, though I live here alone now, happily, as I have for more than two years. And my gratitude is amplified yet again when I realize that within a year or so I will be joined by my new partner, La Conner painter Gray Foster, who will occupy the painting side of the studio, bringing to her work this same sense of commitment and gratitude. Here together, we will accomplish our "mature work," whatever that may come to mean.

But this hermitage should not be misconstrued to mean a retreat from the cares of the world. Quite to the contrary, this hermitage or studio is also a heritage. With Tu Fu and Carruth and Snyder and Levertov and so many other poets, I feel a profound sense of social obligation and a concomitant political commitment. I have written at length (in *At Home in the World* and *A Poet's Work*) on the political significance of poetry and poets as well as on rights and nonviolence. One writes, I suppose, one kind of poetry at the age of twenty-five, another at fifty. Nevertheless, I remain convinced, as I was half a lifetime ago, that even the erotic lyric has profound political ramifications, and that art itself is indelibly stamped with the handprint of suffering humanity. Art is a political act, even in its attempt to hold politics at bay. The building of Kage-an is a political as well as spiritual act. As is the building of a church. I've noted before that one way to write the word *poetry* in Chinese or Japanese combines the characters for "word" and "temple," so that the meaning might be said to be "a temple of words."

It is right, moving into this new studio twenty years after founding Copper Canyon Press, less than a year after burying my adoptive mother, the autumn of my fiftieth year—it is right to reflect and evaluate. But I am also aware that every autobiography is an act of self-justification of a very high order, and this testament or assessment cannot be otherwise.

It is mysterious and beautiful, this sense of beginning a last life. Like Tu Fu, I have had my "long white beard" since my twenties; I am delighted with the passing of each year; I have survived wars, personal and public; have, to echo Pound, "beaten out my exile."

We whose art is accomplished in solitude do not inhabit true solitude, however. Our medium is the spoken word, and the spoken word requires ears and a "clear attentive mind." When, in public schools, I have told children that I spend a lot of time hanging out with old dead guys, they have laughed. But it is true that I find true companionship in the poetry of George Seferis or Paulus Silentiarius, T'ao Ch'ien or Basho. I turn to them for critical eyes: What would Basho say about this line? I turn to them for guidance. They are a very real presence in my solitude.

Here in the comfortable silence of Kage-an, I sit at my desk and write. Coffee steams in my cup. A faint hum from the computer competes with my tinnitus (perpetual ringing in the ears). A rabbit passes through. A deer peruses the garden. Blue jays play at the feeder. Nevertheless, with every sentence I write, I know that somewhere in the world, Salman Rushdie writes under a sentence of death. I know that a modern-day Tu Fu writes out of hunger in exile or in prison. I know that a Jacobo Timerman is tortured for bearing witness.

Nearly fifteen years ago, in a writing workshop at McNeil Island Correctional Facility, my friend Alex told a fellow inmate, "We don't have time for no pity-poor-me poems, man. You're in prison now. The only poem I want to read is the poem you write tonight if tomorrow's your day." All these years later, his words return, demanding conscience, forthrightness, mindfulness.

It all coheres. For me, it begins here, a few miles outside Port Townsend. When my marriage to Tree Swenson ended, I seriously considered leaving Port Townsend and the press; I thought long and hard about teaching, although I remain unlettered. But where could I go and feel at home after twenty years in the misty woods near Port Townsend? I have made my life out of work I've done here. This is my greatest joy, my blissful penury. Like Su Tung-p'o, I try to master the arts of poverty.

It begins here, where a lifetime first began to take shape after imagining a press that publishes great poetry; in the imagining of a house, a garden, a studio; in the years of daily labor and daily meditation: this is the life I have made. The press, under a mostly new staff, begins another life; I begin another life. And yet it is one life. And that life is centered in the economy of the gift, surviving in the margins of free enterprise. I live in the economic shadowlands of this nation because my work has little value in the marketplace. And that which has great value in the marketplace is of little use to me. Someone once remarked to W. H. Auden, "There's no money in poetry." To which Auden replied, "There's no poetry in money, either." The true commerce of poetry is spiritual rather than material, so much so that even the published book is of little use without a disciplined breath and ear and attentive mind to lift the words from the page.

For the middle-aged artist who has been fortunate enough to have enjoyed some modest success, the struggle is to overcome the ugly dragons of complacency. It is easy to find some kind of poem or tune or painting that garners a little praise and then repeat the technique again and again. I distrust the poetry of wit and the "poetic" in general. I do not see the soul of the human eye reflected in the eye of the blue jay that now explores the garden; rather, I see a blue jay. He is a particular blue jay. He has a particular blue-jay disposition. He is a miraculous, temporal embodiment of *blue-jayness*. We are each made of meat and bone, and we are each in this world. As a poet, I search for—as Seamus Heaney once wrote—"the music of what is."

As if the water would answer, I go on talking.
I am telling the waves the story of my days,
I am entering my plea at the tribunal of the sea,
walking alone along the beach at Kalaloch.

Here I once made love with a woman I adored
while a lonely figure watched from bluffs high above,
and the gray implacable tide drew away
to meet the gray implacable sky.

Our cries—love or death—were drowned
by the cries of wandering gulls. Now a year
has passed. And still he is there, watching
from the shadows, sighing the sighs of the sea.

Memory, like waves. Stained with the salts of desire,
a shoreline creature talking fear away,
I go on confessing to the water, understanding
only that the final sentence is death,

a mist falling over the moon,
that is the signature of all things,
beautiful and empty
as the solitary seed syllable of the loon.

SAM HAMILL is a strong-minded, tough, honest poet who sets high standards for himself. He is the founding editor of Copper Canyon Press, which has been located in Port Townsend, Washington, since 1974. An energetic writer, he has published dozens of books of essays, poetry, and translations of poetry.

◇

Hamill's youth was one of literary training alternating with abuse by his adoptive parents and the hell-raising that comes of striking back. He began composing poems at the age of five. His parents were interested in the Romantic poets, and poetry was spoken and read in the home. "I was apparently badly abused as an infant and was so afraid of the dark they had to read to me for long periods each night so I could get to sleep," he remembers. "So I thank them for the poetry, but not for the physical abuse and denial of self-worth that came with it."

Hamill was neither a good nor an interested student, but he discovered that if he did a little extra work he could know more than his teachers on some things. He was kicked out of junior high school for reading Kerouac and eventually, under the influence of the Beats and a general sense of alienation, he became a

street kid that neither his parents nor the courts could stop. "I played pool, hit the road at fourteen, went to San Francisco, and did heroin. Periodically I went, or was sent, home. I wanted to be a beatnik writer but usually was in jail somewhere. I had an extensive record of car theft—seventeen autos—and was busted for drugs and being a runaway."

Told that if he enlisted in the Marine Corps for four years, his record would be cleared, Hamill joined at seventeen. He decided to go to Asia because he had heard of Zen from the beatniks. He landed in Okinawa in 1961.

But the presence of the American military had transformed the island. "The sin culture devastated that population," Hamill says. "There were two kinds of people: those who made money on drugs and prostitution, and the starving farmers. There was no middle class. My first Zen teacher there made me aware of the rich vs. the poor. I began to read Camus and the existentialists, too, and decided not to be a part of the problem anymore. After two years I became a conscientious objector. I said I wouldn't kill for the military, God, or country."

Hamill became a clerk and finished his enlistment because he could not quit. Back home, he entered Los Angeles Valley College and eventually edited the school's newspaper and literary magazine. From there he went on to the University of California at Santa Barbara, where he was "a total misfit."

"I wanted to study with [Asian literature scholars] Kenneth Rexroth and Hugh Kenner but was kicked out of the Creative Studies program. I was not a grad nor an undergrad student and pissed off everybody. My dissertation would have been on Ezra Pound and the Chinese poets."

Hamill edited the literary magazine *Spectrum* but was fired, he asserts, "for the crime of not publishing faculty members." Still, he earned the Coordinating Council of Literary Magazines' Editor's Award for "producing the best journal in the country." He took the award money, five hundred dollars, moved to Colorado, and founded Copper Canyon Press in 1972.

He had begun translating poetry at Los Angeles Valley College, an endeavor that led him to teach himself the rudiments of several languages. He first translated the Spanish-language poets Federico Garcia Lorca and Pablo Neruda. "I tried to find an English equivalent for the incantatory power of the best of them. I wasn't interested in academic definitions of translation. For example, in Chinese classical poetry, when they found a word that didn't make sense in English, they used the literal translation with a footnote. That is scholarship, not poetry. I wanted to say things straighter, in a more lyrical way, and get away from academic translatorese."

Hamill's study was exploratory. He learned Latin by teaching himself to translate Catullus. After preliminary work on Chinese classical poetry, he turned to Japanese,

discovering along the way that the work of the great poet Basho was influenced by the Chinese master Tu Fu.

In spirituality, besides Tu Fu, Hamill claims the most kinship with the Zen poets Basho, Ryokan, and Ikkyu. His translation of Basho's acclaimed *Oku no Hosomichi* was published by Shambhala during the Gulf War. "It was a cherished moment for me; it has beautiful antiwar poems in it, and the Gulf War represented everything despicable about government, racism, classism, and genocide."

◊

Hamill's work also involved teaching in prisons from 1976 to 1988, conducting two-week, intensive creative writing workshops. "In prison, we created a Socratic dialogue with the inmates," he says. "There was absolute confidentiality, which meant that for many, for the first time in their lives, we sat down nose-to-nose with truth. Eighty-seven percent of the more than a million men in American prisons are high school dropouts, and ninety percent of them were battered or abused children. I asked them for an honest self-assessment and encouraged them to begin changing what they didn't like."

Known for his public statements, Hamill says he may be the first writer to speak out in public as a reformed batterer himself. "My warts have been out there since day one," he says with a laugh.

◊

Hamill spent four years during the 1970s building his house near Port Townsend. He has spent several years since creating a viewing garden and has recently completed a new building that combines writing and painting studios.

But it is his depth of influence on behalf of nonviolence and feminist issues in the context of his own dharma practice that he is most proud of. Hamill has, for a quarter century, consistently worked on behalf of domestic violence and sexual assault programs. He served on the board of directors of the Jefferson County Domestic Violence/Sexual Assault Program for four years. "Like hammering nails," he says, "it's right work, right mindfulness."

Fragments from Driving: This Is Their Place

Sharon Doubiago

The very dust upon which you now stand responds more lovingly to footsteps [of my people] than to yours, because it is rich with the blood of our ancestors and our feet are conscious of the sympathetic touch.

—Chief Seattle, Suquamish Tribe

TUESDAY, 7 P.M., BRANSCOMB ROAD

Dirt. Steep ridge. Clearcuts both sides from sea to crest. Sun setting in the ocean behind me. All the world coral pinks and black shadows of stumps.

This is their place.

And what we did to them and their place is our hell now, our karma, why our marriages don't survive, why our children are so tormented, why we die of cancer, why we are all bound for home-lessness.

I return to my mother's place in Florence, Oregon, for my journals and files on living in the Northwest, after three and a half months in Mendocino, California (the southern boundary of the Northwest), six weeks of which have been on the streets and bluffs in my van, Psyche. I return because if I write this essay I am guaranteed two thousand dollars in the next year, the first thousand, I'm assured, as soon as I sign the contract. This is good money for a poet—though not much in 1993–94 for anyone for whom it is the only scheduled income. But this has been my pattern for thirteen years. Having established residency the length of the U.S. Pacific Coast—but mainly in the Northwest—that is, having acquired friends and knowledge of many of its amazing places, both natural and cultural, I go where I can write, where I am wanted, where the next paycheck is.

Labor Day, my first weekend in Psyche, I was hassled by the state park rangers for my trash in their cans. *Alice's Restaurant!* I get a lot of mail (c/o General Delivery). Where am I to throw what I can't save? I eat in my van—where am I to throw their irreducible packaging? Just part of the most current campaign to rid the streets, that is, the eyes of the still-housed, of the truth of their country.

One night they stopped my son in his van, Gi-hugest. Looking at his Utah license, they asked if his mom lives in a van with Oregon plates.

So many times I knew their binoculars were on me.

"Someday," Paul, another van-dwelling artist, said after we were hassled for still being on the bluffs five minutes after the sun went down, "the American people are going to wake up and realize what they've allowed to happen."

Such faith he has—even for his Iroquois-African heritage.

My friends and family voice concern for me. They're afraid of the robbers and rapists. Most of the time it's the cops I'm afraid of.

But even so, I still feel safest on the road, with wheels under me, a motor for driving away. When I'm in a house, with a known address, I feel a sitting duck. I *have* been a sitting duck. "A moving target," the San Francisco–Sierra poet Lew Welch said, "is hard to hit."

I haven't paid rent since 1980—maybe six months total in the thirteen years. The exceptional two months this summer were paid by my mother so my daughter *y nieto* could come home from Paris, and Mama, in search of a nontoxic environment, could try out Mendocino. Mi hijo, too—all of us under one roof.

"*When my children left home I made the decision not to work in order to pay rent in order to write.*" I needed to write full-time. I wanted to go deeper into the values I had taught them—*remain true to yourself, follow your dreams, love the others, love the Earth, money isn't everything, a good life's possible without it, maybe impossible with it.*

My "house," Psyche, is a 1977 slant-six Dodge van, given to me by my parents in November 1981 when they grasped that I was living in Roses, my 1969 Ambassador Motors station wagon. "We didn't pay for your college education, so now you must accept this gift." I live in Psyche because I want to know the Northwest. (*I want to enter it, to be one with it. We are here. That is all we know. I want to know where we are.*) I live in the Northwest because it is the least developed place in the United States; only here, I suspect, could I have lived in Psyche for thirteen years. I live this way rather than as a landowner because even as a "good" one, "landlady" would pollute the spirit I most want to cultivate. "One doesn't sell the land the people walk upon," Crazy Horse said. I live this way to better know the ancient Vision of the people whose place this is. I picture the wide-open spaces of the Southwest and see I am too visible, my Psyche in all that light, silhouetted on all those horizons.

THIS IS THEIR PLACE: MENDOCINO

I found a significantly large group of people who had come at the end of the Sixties, early part of the Seventies. You heard about this back-to-the-land movement in the media many years ago . . . then never anything more about it. Did the movement thrive? Did it even survive? What I found is that these people are still up there. They have schools—high schools as well as home schooling. They have a spectrum of alternative forms of education, they have their alternative kinds of relationships. They have home births. And they are very active in all kinds of environmental issues.

It came to me: this is what makes northern California unique . . . these alternative lifestyles that people have tried out . . . and evolved. That a lot of people who came twenty, twenty-five years back are still there. And the ideals and lifestyles that they came with, or started or tried, have evolved . . .

—Phil Shermeister, "The Story National Geographic Squashed,"
The New Settler Interview, August 1993

I have always taken Melville's "It is not down on any map; true places never are," to mean maps don't tell you where the true places are.

By Mendocino I do not mean the tourist place of boutiques. The true place of Mendocino stretches from the Gualala to the Mattole on Cape Mendocino. It stretches over the Coast Range to, in some places, the Interstate 5 corridor, though Highway 101 is its more common eastern border. The heart of the place is somewhere between the Navarro and Noyo rivers.

My mother says we went through the village of Mendocino in 1950 and as we left, crossing Big River, I looked back and said, "When I grow up I'm going to live there."

Mendocino. The only place I have ever been where the dominant paradigm is, To thine own self be true. Rather than as with everywhere else, To those in power (social and psychological) be true. As a result, Mendocino is surely the most politically radical, psychologically evolved place of white folks on the planet.

I could never have become myself without the long, healing, still-unfolding process that is Mendocino.

. . . I love Mendocino because it is feminine. I have heard men describe it as feminine. It is often compared with Big Sur, which is "masculine." If it is true that the Muse is feminine, then perhaps this is why I found my voice here, in the fog and dark and layers of bluffs and ridges and redwoods, the soft golden light so erotic on the skin, and the ocean everywhere . . .

. . . I understand more here. I understand less. The Mystery is confronted continuously . . . "How a tree feels . . . that's when you write a poem, when you know how a tree feels . . ." I live here because everything lends its consciousness to every other thing. You can almost hear the conversations of plants, of whales, of deer.

. . . I live here for the water. Images float on it, by it, through it? Electrical currents? I don't know, but people become poets when they move here because they start remembering. I live here for the clarity of my dreams and the dreams of others, how I fall into their sleep waves and dreamtides, finding form, narrative, structure to the deep sea of my thoughts, to what I could never make into comprehensible shape before. I live here because I can know the stories of others—I can see the song of the land, the stories being received and written into their bodies . . . In this place I have come to know a truth I denied before: the living spirit needs story for its survival and renewal . . . I have learned here that craft is spiritual.

And when I looked west again
to that desolate islet
I saw the massacred coming back . . .

Those made of this coast
pushed out
to the last, barren, most western rock

where they fled
*16 men, women, and children**

11 P.M.

Passing up the Klamath River turnoff so not going to Ashland, at least my favorite way, through the Yuroks, the Hupas, the Karuks, the people who have *always* been there.

Within a circle whose radius is approximately six miles, with Weithcpec as the center, three of the six major linguistic groups recognized in North America come into contact.

Hokan. Algonquian. Athabascan.

NORTH OF TRINIDAD

I was planning to sleep on the beach south of Crescent City, but now this dark rest stop, this great redwood, an old-growth stump from which grows a circle of many old second growths, is irresistible.

The redwoods once covered all of North America, Greenland, Europe, and Iceland. Now only this logged stretch of northern California and the Sierras, one small patch in China.

In bed, Giovanni. Coming down from Oregon. Two nights in B&Bs, my first ever in Mendocino. (I washed all my clothes in the bathtub of the Victorian Farmhouse, just as I did years ago when I lived there.) And now I'm always walking into the Albion River Inn, being hit by the money folks, the clean folks, the pampered and self-pampered. Shocking, coming straight from the streets and bluffs. *Their noses in the air,* that expression, that classic look of arrogance, I saw that they really did have

---

* The Goat Rock Massacre was perpetrated in March 1843 by Salvador Vallejo's army, which chased the Staiyomis Indians of the Sonoma area to Goat Rock, where the Staiyomis were joined by "the Indians of the region around Mendocino Bay." Some accounts place the number killed much higher.

their collective noses slightly elevated in the surf-pounded, oxygenated atmosphere. Then, on every wave rushing though the bluffs into the Albion's mouth, while I tried to get the pasta into mine, was one of the homeless men I'd been sharing the streets with. Mostly men, mostly middle-aged—one young woman, Indian, a few young men—all filthy, starving, ragged. One guy especially, who props himself on Main Street in front of the duck pond with the sign AGING HIPPY IN NEED OF LOVE. The morning Giovanni was to arrive I suddenly saw how much thinner he was than at the beginning of the summer. As we drank expensive Mendocino wine, all September's sky and sea and earth, the days and nights, the moon and stars and sun, washed in and out the tides of my every cell.

Hard being inside. Hard not to bolt.

I tried to explain. He took classic offense, told me of his priest's sermon. When they come to his door "for handouts, having cruised over to the coast though they can't get back," he gives them "a little gas money and a big lecture, 'You know damn well the only jobs are in the valley; what are you doing here?'"

It's not just the money that makes it nearly impossible to get back; it's what happens to you psychologically, experiences unimaginable to the Housed. You know their lies so overwhelmingly that even if you regard yourself as a total victim, helpless at the feet of a system you'd love to get back into, your spirit has been living the truth of the culture. No matter their "prayers" for your soul, you have become Sasquatch, one with the despoiled land, one of the Genocided, kicked-out; at best, Reservationed.

The sun set in our faces. I saw Thelma and Louise at the wheel, staring into the Grand Canyon, the cops behind them ready to "rehabilitate" them. "Go for it!" The words just blew out of my mouth in the Ashland theater. It's the only suicide I've ever cheered.

"The only way," I tried to explain to this generous man who loves me but doesn't understand me, "to know the worlds you aren't living is through the spiritual. This is what priests are for. Not poisoning the minds of the congregation. 'Knock and ye shall receive!'"

And obviously I took Jesus too seriously as a child.

Falling asleep, hands down my sides, me too, skinny again. Back in my mother's mirrors I'll be sexy and fashionable.

Groups of armed assassins roamed the area of the Northwest. From 1850 to 1870, nearly 20,000 people were killed.

—Jack Norton, Genocide in Northwestern California

Waking in the night, so dark these woods, that steep hill out my front window Sasquatch. Ishi. (Why don't they realize that hounding the homeless only makes their rest stops less safe for them?)

This is their place. The Ones Who Didn't Have Mirrors. Who knew themselves in bodies of water, in the shade the sun casts from behind, in the Eyes of the Others.

Chilula. The Redwood People.

ROAD SCHOLAR

To be ignorant of what happened before you were born is to be forever a child.

—Cicero, 108–43 B.C.

Being on the road is research. I'm a scholar by nature, a digger of the truth by temperament. This passion is inherited from my parents, was deeply nourished by them, those kids who birthed me a year to the day after they left the South in a getaway car, three hundred years after the first members of their European sides arrived on Turtle Island's shores. (The Cherokee, Choctaw, and Seminole are of my mother's side.) After I left home, my parents became real estate brokers in Ramona. "One doesn't sell the land," Crazy Horse, Sequoia, and every Native American across this vast continent has said. But my parents loved the land and were honest, conscientious, and determined to survive with "*self-respect.*" Daddy loved to "locate" the properties, often difficult in those desert mountains, by walking off the boundaries. Mama, my orphan, found homes for people.

Not long after the Modoc Wars of 1872–73, the Pit River people were rounded up . . . Some were herded to Eureka where they boarded a ship, after being assured many times they would be transported to a land where there were no killings or no white men with guns . . . Many were happy to go, happy to get away from "civilization."

The U.S. government then . . . transported the people out to the ocean . . .

—*Genocide in Northwestern California*

THIS IS THEIR PLACE: PORT TOWNSEND

(Port Townsend originally was "Dalmo'ma," a Pit River place name meaning "digging for roots." It is also the name of the anthology of "literature and responsibility" published by Empty Bowl Press in Port Townsend.)

May 8, 1981, Sam Hamill's Thirty-Ninth Birthday Party:
David Romtvedt said he could never understand the artist Mark Rothko. His paintings were just these big rectangles of plain color. But at the exhibit he saw that "*the line between the two colors vibrated, wildly, where they came together, the interface creating a whole other reality.*

"This is like the poetry here. When I first came from the University of Iowa I couldn't understand the scene here at all. I couldn't read Sam, at all! And McNulty was okay, but I always felt, So what? Now I begin to see it. *The interface between the poems and the place vibrates.*"

As we talked, my eyes fell on the watercolor on the opposite wall. The palest blue wash, a swirl suggesting a cloud or a sail or a bird or a big wave (but there aren't big waves here). I felt the many miles I had walked in the past twenty-four hours. I saw again the beautiful horses on Hastings Road standing in puddles of water, the pastures and fields and woods behind them so green as to elicit the adjective "profound." I thought *horses running off as water.*

The aesthetic here is *blending in.* Never a loud bursting within or without the form (though St. Helens is going off again this very minute as I write) . . . In the mythology of Wicca, *north* is crystallization, north is silence, the voice frozen. I think we are lucky with these frozen throats to get *any* words (wash) from here.

July 1981, Fort Worden. "The sorrow of the distance between the narrator and the world" (poet Robert Hass).

Jim Heynen said to me today, "The Klallam hated anything that was beautiful." "Ha!" I laughed. "That's still the way it is with the locals." "I know," he said.

I think they hated beauty for the reasons the Fascists loved it, murdered for it. *"Beauty"* not only stands out, it stands above.

I live here because there's no electricity. My body attunes itself to the moon. My bleeding so deep, so rhythmic, the blood of joy.

> *Cedar is a poem about writing*
> *cut and nailed*
> *beyond your white freckled shoulders*
>
> *the falling light*
>
> *of your light curls*
> *our ceiling*
>
> > *"Is it that we are halfway*
> > *between the North Pole and the equator?*
> > *Less than*
> > *two hundred miles north*
> > *of the 45th Parallel?*
> > *Is this why*
> >
> > *their poems are quiet, balanced*
> > *rectangles?"*
> >
> > *"Actually," he sighs, "they are*
> > *squares."*

Cedar is a poem about writing
the squares, the logos
of Northwest Indian art

across your shoulders
up your

totem

> (*Anyone who's taken the bus*
> *to the Equator knows:*
> *The 45th Parallel*
> > *that far again*
> > > *to the North Pole.*

> "*The difficulty,*" *he says*
> "*with the theory of the 45th Parallel*
> *is it includes the south of France and*
> *Montana.*"

> "*But this is where*
> *longitude comes in. The exact*

> *place*"

> (*the water color of your tears*
> > *the rain coming down*
> > > *this point washed in sorrow*
> > > *this bluff*
> > > > *of their tears*

In 1991 Denise Levertov makes a similar effort to describe Far Northwest poetry, "the deep spiritual longing" that "gives rise to a more conscious attentiveness to the non-human and to a more or less conscious desire to immerse *the self in the larger whole*—that element I have called the spiritual quest . . . Such poems communicate not just the appearance of phenomena but the presence of spirit *within* those phenomena. I have referred to an Asian influence, but *the assumption of such spiritual presence in landscape is even more closely related to Native American beliefs*" (*New and Selected Essays*, emphasis mine).

One day in November 1980, when I first moved into the rent-free Puma Bluff cabin with the poet Michael Daley, I read a story in the Seattle paper of a woman my age who had driven from New York to the northwesternmost point of the United States looking for a new life, the same Fourth of July week I drove to Port Townsend from Mendocino. She left her car and hiked, with provisions for several days, around Cape Flattery, and then south. Now, in November, her body had been found, raped and beaten to death.

In my psyche, my nightmares, she is the girl inside who didn't make it, one of my soul sisters on the road, this journey I've just begun.

And one Sunday (*September 9, 1990*) in Port Townsend, I spent the afternoon with Martin Charles. "I'm the only living, full-blooded Port Townsend Klallam left." He showed me the exact spot where he was born, in 1915, "in the hole," now the high school football and baseball field. "We played fireball."

The Klallam village at Port Townsend, Kah Tai, was burned to the ground August 31, 1871, "by a contingent of soldiers from Fort Townsend."

— "Shadows of Our Ancestors," *Dalmo'ma VIII*

WEDNESDAY MORNING, OCTOBER 13, 1993

Foggy. Rained in the night.

In and out of blue redwood. A cross on the road.

When Daddy was dying, the final stages, in the living room overlooking the Siuslaw River in Florence's sand dunes, I was haunted with wanting to know *who else left from this very spot?* I figured time and place, September 18, 1987, predicted his last breath, 1:21 P.M.

The science of astronomy is based on the mathematical conjunctions of places and times. Astrology is the interpretation—the "abstract"— of the story of these points, where the two come together, from thirty thousand years of continuous study (i.e., Tibetan astrology), a study that was advanced before we came so permanently indoors, before we became "abstract thinkers." Astrology is a highly physical science, though many astrologers don't realize this.

If we have past lives, our old bodies are buried in places all around the earth.
Time loops back on itself like dough being kneaded.

MOUTH OF THE SMITH RIVER

Yontoket. Here for thousands of years the Tolowa people prayed and conducted their religious ceremonies. This is their Center of the World . . . In the fall of 1853, the Tolowas gathered at Yontoket. Citizens from Crescent City formed a "company," and dressing like soldiers, . . . ringed the sacred village . . . Over four hundred and fifty people were murdered . . .

— Genocide in Northwestern California

(*The Oregonian*, 1853: "The whole Indian race of southern Oregon must be exterminated.")

Borders.

Growing up looking south into Mexico, west into the Pacific.

When I was a teenager, there was the campaign to close the border to us. Years of headlines, horror stories, their fear tactics to save us from the Unknowns making racists of us instead. Prejudice is a border phenomenon, why bordering countries are so astonishingly different from each other. *England, France, Germany, Italy, Spain.* Just north of Mendocino: Fort Bragg (Fort Drag). North of Ashland: Medford (Dreadford). East of Eugene: Springfield (anti-gay Oregon Citizens Alliance!).

I come back to the place William Stafford has just left. I last read with him in June in Lake Oswego. He *was* old and visibly weakened. Michael Daley used to say, "That guy has a dark side, a sinister side, even, that others don't see." Daley told him this that night in Port Townsend's Sea Galley. "Yes!" Stafford shouted, seeming relieved.

Sun out in Gold Beach! Just like the brochures brag—"the Banana Belt" (just like the Sequim, Washington, one boasts). Spectacularly clear, the blue and white Pacific, rows and rows of white foaming waves churning in.

There's the logging road up the Rogue over the Siskiyous and the Klamaths. Range after range of clearcuts.

THIS IS THEIR PLACE: ASHLAND

In the north shadow of Mount Shasta (held by white tradition as the West Coast's most powerful psychic place) and just south of the Oregon Vortex in Gold Hill, Ashland is as much a healing capital as a theater one—*oh surely, there are more healers and psychics there per square mile than any place on the continent!* Lithium is a natural product in the water (thus Lithia Creek and Park); in the early white days Ashland developed as a resort. In the early fifties, after repeated crashes of planes approaching the Medford airport, the FAA finally conceded that the cause was the Vortex, and though "unexplainable," instructed pilots to adjust their instruments accordingly. Gold Hill is at the apex of magnetic gridlines mapped to Monterey Bay (and through the planet to the Bermuda Triangle and the seven other major planetary vortexes). In the Real Days of the Takilma, it was a main restorative place of the whole West Coast for men (while Wilbur Springs of the Yawisel, now of Mendocino, was the spiritual center for women of tribes as far north as Shasta). In the sixties and seventies Ashland was another hub for the back-to-the-land folks. But despite its fame for productions of William Shakespeare, the most recognized poet of Western

Civ, Ashland has been a hard place to be a poet. Lately, though, they've been coming down out of the hills.

When man and the world become unbalanced, then we must dance the great dances, rhythmically stomping upon the earth, exchanging with it and balancing all that brings health, strength, food, honor, good luck, and happiness for all.

—Genocide in Northwestern California

I live in these towns because I can dance every night! *Skipping 2 A.M. down the back alleys after dancing to great rock 'n' roll (Robert Cray and Curtis Salgado in Ashland in the early eighties), the freedom at long last of the boy.*

I live in these towns because it's relatively safe to be out at night unattended.

The cultural choices are so rich in towns like Mendocino, Ashland, Port Townsend, you have to "pace yourself." In the cities you have to make *appointments* for everything, even nature, even love. But in these towns, daily, just to walk down the street is to run into some of the best writers, musicians, actors, thinkers, painters, printers, potters, sculptors, healers, alternative livers, politicos on the planet.

But sometimes, in Ashland especially, the hypocrisy is awful. Walking those hills and streets as I have now for twelve years, I've felt the presence of the former people stronger than in most places.

> *Flesh*
> *of their bodies we call*
> *real estate. Breath*
> *of their decomposing*

They, however, and what happened to them, are not acknowledged.

That a town so hip, so tuned into the psychic, to the spiritual, to healing, so into Indian symbolism and ceremony, could be in such blatant denial; that a town with a collective philosophy of "all is unfolding as it should" (*all's well that ends well*), that the hells are just a state of mind or the final upheaval of the Old World, that the New World is at hand and we are it—well, to believe that we will survive, wonderfully, when they died horribly, is an elitism and racism that pull the rug out from under any true New Age gains. Likewise, to deny the negative impact money has on the psyche, as do most of the expensive healers there, is— immoral. It is precisely hypocrisy that allows, indeed *encourages*, the killings. "This is why liberals are the most hated," Tom Chamberlin, the Portland filmmaker, said to me this summer. "They are the most dishonest." In this way, even the Ashland soul is one with the American soul, "a killer" (D. H. Lawrence).

As real healers know, you cannot get well until you fully acknowledge the past.

In the spring of 1981, one of my first nights in Ashland, sleeping in the basement of my sister's church on East Main, I dreamed I was an old woman tending bar at a lodge on Crater Lake. I had not been to Crater Lake since I was nine, though I knew it was somewhere northeast of Ashland. I had never dreamed myself old (and never have again). So, though I am a coastal person, not a mountain one, ever since then I've sent my soulmates postcards of Crater Lake with the message, *If we lose each other, look for me here.*

April 26, 1992, a ceremony in the Mark Antony Hotel to exorcise the place of its curse—it's built on top of a burial ground! (I want to scream, *So it'll make money?*) Agnes Taowhywee Pilgrim introduces herself as the lone surviving full-blooded Takilma. "The State of Oregon says I don't exist, but I have all the papers to prove it." Her father was the first chief of the Seletz Confederacy, her grandfather a warrior who signed the Rogue River Wars Peace Treaty.

NORTH MOUTH OF THE ROGUE RIVER, ROAD SIGN:

SEVERE FIGHTING TOOK PLACE IN CURRY COUNTY DURING THE LAST ROGUE RIVER INDIAN WAR. IN MARCH 1856 A COMPANY OF MINUTEMEN, 34 STRONG, WERE BESIEGED IN AN IMPROVISED FORTIFICATION OF LOGS BY A LARGE FORCE OF PISTOL RIVER AND ROGUE RIVER INDIANS. THE INDIANS, CONTRARY TO THEIR USUAL CUSTOM, REPEATEDLY CHARGED WITH DESPERATE COURAGE. THE SIEGE INVOLVING HAND-TO-HAND FIGHTING WAS CARRIED ON FOR SEVERAL DAYS UNTIL THE INDIANS WERE FINALLY DISPERSED.

1 P.M., PORT ORFORD, BATTLE ROCK

> *The high-reaching sun-glistening wave's*
> *first folding over*
> *its underside of green (glass)*
>
> *lap, lip, first*
> *kiss! Most exquisite*
>
> *moment*

Surely, the ocean has structured my poetics more than any other factor.

1:30 P.M., BANDON

Bandon always makes me think "abandon." *To be abandoned. To have abandon. To undo the bands. Bonds.*

Living this way also has been part of freeing myself of the unhealthy love patterns of my culture. When a man treats me wrong I walk out the door to Psyche, *quick as that.*

But sometimes the loneliness is terrible. The sense of being cut off, abandoned, in exile from the Main Land.

And truck drivers? That guy in *Thelma and Louise* was mild. Oh, I could tell truck driver stories . . .

And it's the Interstate 5 corridor through the Willamette Valley where men pass you in their little cars with their erect penises exposed.

2:00 P.M., COOS BAY

When I lived in Vermont a woman from this town
was sentenced first to death and then to life
in a Turkish prison for smuggling hashish.
Across the sub-zero hillside of northern Appalachia
came the sunbluffs and islets, the white-ribboned blue Pacific
of Coos Bay. And a prison wall without windows.
I heard the sentence so that everything started
and the beaches of my childhood
came through the courtroom haze
and my body was breaking open
the story I'd never live.

The Coo people are peaceful. But the U.S. Army marched us from Coos Bay to Yachats. No food at Yachats. Beaten at the agency, exposed to the weather. Starved. Ran into the sea. Drowned. In five years half were dead at Yachats. The survivors cleared the land, farmed. In 1875 the whites took the land at Yachats.

—Annie Minor Peterson, age 70, the last surviving
Coo-speaking person, statement recorded in the 1930s,
broadcast on KOAC radio, 1993

2:45 P.M., FLORENCE

This place Daddy last breathed, left. *44 degrees by 124 degrees 7 minutes.* (How to understand the degree of its small Republican heart?) We played him all the versions we could find of "Amazing Grace," his favorite song. He loved to tell the story of the preacher who wrote it, a captain of a ship carrying slaves to America. Halfway across the Atlantic he was struck by the Vision: *This is wrong.* Turned the ship back to Africa, returned the people home.

First I was blind. Then I saw. Amazing grace, for a wretch like me.

Florence, *"named for a board washed from halfway around the world,"* named for the greatest art city of the Western world, is a town of no art. "Un-*named in Sometimes a Great Notion,*" the town on which Kesey based his outrageous story. At night in the bars in Old Town the outrageousness is still there: the bikers, old hippies, fishers, loggers, the ones who pride themselves on *never* going over to the valley, hard-drinking businessmen and retirees, mill and construction workers, and down-and-outers, the ones too hurt to return to their famous careers or, simply, to Southern California. I sit in Fisherman's Wharf and know that if I had sat here as a young woman I would have become a painter: the calling of my soul to render the outrageous faces across this horseshoe bar.

"The Siuslaw? None left. All interbred with the whites."

I come back to my mother, living outside her third toxic home in four years. In the first house, which she built in Ashland after Daddy's death, it was the formaldehyde. Formaldehyde ("*a colorless, pungent gas,* CH_2O") is a Northwest tree product. It's the "glue" that holds "civilization" together. With her second house it was Ashland's air, the eighteen formaldehyde-spewing mill stacks of Medford. This third house should have been obvious, but for her panic: a mobile home.

So my mother walks the beach every day. To breathe oxygen. And searches for an old house on the sand.

My mother, Garnet Audrey Clarke Edens, great-great-great-grandchild of William Rogers Clark, who with Meriwether Lewis, Sacajawea, Jean Baptist *et al.* spent the 1805–1806 winter on Oregon's beach, the orphan who taught me to love America and its land, who has done it "the way you're supposed to," magnificently, heroically, is once again, as she was as a child, homeless.

When I was a girl she often mused that she was born in the wrong century, how much she wished she could have come west in a covered wagon on the Oregon Trail, "to better know the land." In 1988 we found her mother's grave, SUSAN SIMMONS CLARKE, 1900–1924, just beneath the Danville, Virginia, state line in North Carolina. Dead of the tuberculosis that swept through the Dan River Cotton Mill. Mama, who was four years and three weeks old at her burial, had not been aware until I pointed to it, kneeling over my twenty-four-year-old grandmother, surprising tears spewing out, that the cemetery road is named *Oregon*.

SHARON DOUBIAGO is a writer of the West Coast—the entire West Coast. From San Diego to Port Townsend she has loved its wild waves and rocks; she has lived for months at a time in her van, skirting the law, and is now researching the history of the coast's original peoples. As a poet and writer, she is controversial, intense, and passionate about loving men, supporting women, and raising children. She has published five books of poetry, stories, and essays, including two book-length epic poems.

◊

Doubiago was once what she calls a "Bible scholar." Her family lived in South Central Los Angeles, and from ages seven to twelve she embraced the neighborhood's Trinity Bible Baptist Church. "I regard the spiritual experience I had as a child as genuine and profound as any adult's. It initiated the psychic structure that's made me a poet—my prayers to Jesus were my first poems."

Another important factor in her childhood was her exposure to the stream of "broken men" that flowed daily by her tract house, a house situated between residential and industrial areas. From Rancho Los Amigos, the Los Angeles County Farm and Hospital, these men were mostly war veterans, crippled, sick, and insane, on their way to the liquor store.

"The first poem that came out of me, 'Pharisees,' at nineteen, was about them, my neighborhood, and the church. The people in the area ridiculed and tormented them, which, though I was terrified of them too, I hated. 'Love thy neighbor as thyself'—I could feel their suffering. But it wasn't until I wrote the poem, as a class assignment, that I saw the hypocrisy of my beloved church, which never reached out to them."

Doubiago is the eldest of three children. Her parents, Fred and Garnet Edens, had lived in Tennessee, Virginia, and North Carolina before California. Her father worked for Douglas Aircraft, and the family lived in the Lakewood–Long Beach area until his mother died. Then, Doubiago's mother insisted that the family move to the country. They landed in Ramona, in rural San Diego County, and built their own business, a drive-in restaurant called Edens' Heavenly Hamburgers. Doubiago describes her parents as independent, moral, philosophical, and serious about life and the world. "My mother is spiritual, somewhat mystical, but she did not go to church. She always said that's not necessary to know God."

When they moved to Ramona, Doubiago was cut off from her old church, and her religious fervor cooled. At fifteen she met the nineteen-year-old Ukrainian-Russian George Boris Doubiago, a sailor from Long Island, New York. They became secretly engaged. Forbidden to date in high school, they married two weeks after she graduated. They had a son, Daniel, when Sharon was nineteen.

"My mother informed me that she was going to take care of the baby two days a week, that I must find something to do for 'just me.' Otherwise, she said, I would 'lose myself' as she had lost herself when she had three babies in three years. Undoubtedly, this is the greatest gift ever given to me."

Doubiago went to Palomar Community College, then to California State University, Los Angeles, where she earned a master's degree in English. Her daughter, Shawn, was born when she was twenty-two, and when she was twenty-five, she and George divorced.

Doubiago wrote her first stories in junior high school. When she was fifteen, she and her fiancé wrote daily for two and a half years, correspondence she calls "the real beginning of my writing. But I was also writing about him—'The Book of Doubi,' a poem-like thing, about everything I knew about him and everything he meant to me, all in a structure similar to my long poems now, the most natural structure for me. The archetype, I've realized, is the Bible, with its histories, geographies, mythologies, migrations, and many voices and points of view and addresses to God and the people."

Doubiago says the birth of her son marked a turning point in her faith in both religion and her country. "The love I knew for him forced me to question everything I had so deeply believed in and lived as truth. For the next five years I had direct, ongoing confrontation with Christianity, mainly with the issue of good and evil and how this relates to innocent children (and therefore all humanity). If God is God he is not Good. If God is Good he is not God. Archibald MacLeish's refrain from his *J. B.* was a constant in my medita-

tion. In those five years, I birthed two children from a man who did not love me. The civil rights movement and the Vietnam War were happening and I was getting, two days a week, an education.

"God, even Jesus, became too small."

◊

After graduate school, Doubiago vowed "not to be a poet. I was educated by Formalists—the law and order of poetry seemed identical to the law and order of the Army—and knowing nothing else, I accepted that the powerful force inside me was not poetry. I was too female, too working-class, but worst of all, too rhythmic, too emotional, too sexual. And the war and its rhetoric, the hypocritical, racist evil of my government, destroyed any remaining vestiges of belief in language. Language was a lie."

Traveling with her children and a new partner, she spent time in Los Angeles and around the country, often living in the car, rarely paying rent. Doubiago did keep a journal, "almost against my will," which she describes as unreadable, but which she later developed into stories and poems. The language is not personal, like a diary, nor is it "public." "I could not, would not bring a controlling consciousness to it. It was a quest to find my real words and concerns."

They moved to Mendocino in northern California in September 1974. "In October, Anne Sexton killed herself. Less than two weeks later I came out as a poet at an open reading in Elk on the Pacific bluffs. Very soon after that, that 'partner,' the man I'd loved and lived with for nine years, who'd raised my children to teenagers, left—because I had become a poet. My silence, I had to admit then, had been a condition of our relationship."

Five years later, Doubiago and her daughter decided to travel to

Colombia, Ecuador, and Peru. The trip resulted in the celebrated *South America Mi Hija,* a 300-page epic poem published by the University of Pittsburgh Press in 1992. Along with geography, psychology, mythology, politics, and European and American indigenous histories, the book explores the complex issues—and pain—of sexuality and relations between the sexes.

From 1980 to 1985, Doubiago lived mainly in Port Townsend in her van and a rent-free primitive cabin on Puma Bluff. She was a bartender at the Sea Galley restaurant and the Back Alley tavern and was active in the Empty Bowl Press collective. She credits the poetry community there, including Centrum, the annual writers conference to which she first won a scholarship in 1977, as being an important factor in her developing poetics. "I tell beginning poets they must find a poetry community. It is too lonely, too impossible an art to survive otherwise."

After publication of her epic poem *Hard Country* by West End Press in 1983, she began to get temporary teaching jobs as well as invitations and small fees for readings and lectures. *Hard Country* was followed by three books, written mostly in her van: *The Book of Seeing with One's Own Eyes* (Graywolf, 1988) and *El Niño* (Lost Roads, 1989), both autobiographical prose stories, and *Psyche Drives the Coast, Poems 1975–1987* (Empty Bowl), which was awarded the 1991 Hazel B. Hall Oregon Book Award for Poetry.

◊

For the past decade, Doubiago has been writing the story of her son's life as an athlete, and has developed several thousand pages of raw manuscript called *Son,* which he is editing. "*Son* has a similar understanding about gender as does *South America Mi Hija,* but it's prose, has a lot of humor and great stories, some of well-known athletes.

Danny played pro football for five years. I call the book a feminist narrative of raising a male athlete. Our culture prides itself on having examined and broken all the taboos, yet here is this enormous one.

"There are no books, no research, no talking, no looking at the mother/son relationship, no therapy except the Freudian one that legitimizes, indeed encourages, mother-hatred. The main killers in history are eighteen-year-old boys who have just left their mothers—boys seeking male identity, trying to prove they're men, not mama's boys. Boys have to cut themselves from their mothers, from the feminine, to be a man. Because we can't look at the mother/son relationship, women accept that the wise thing to do is to let their sons go."

Published pieces from *Son* have won Doubiago a Northwest Sportswriter of the Year Award and also Tom Robbins's Darrell Bob Houston Annual Award for Journalism.

◊

Doubiago says she took a vow of poverty in her twenties because of what she grasped about capitalism and its destruction of the land and people. "I've written full-time now for twenty years—basically eight to twelve hours a day. There are two novels and hundreds of stories, poems, and essays in draft. And somehow I've managed to travel—though not as extensively as I need to. I really need help. All I really want to do is continue this pattern. But with my daughter a single mother and young writer living in Paris, I need more financial resources."

In the future, Doubiago feels she may take a university teaching position, but not until she has evolved as a poet. "I simply could not have written what I needed to write, under the oppressive codes of academia. But now, with the security of my published books, I think I can do it. Actually, I'm a fine teacher."

Five Poems

William Stafford

Editor's note: William Stafford died suddenly during the preparation of this anthology. He had sent warm and enthusiastic letters and examples of the type of poems he would include in his contribution to this book. In the spirit of his wish to be included in an anthology that addressed the land and writers of his beloved Northwest, we include his preliminary draft. We have reprinted the works he sent, as well as an essay about him written by his son Kim R. Stafford, a noted Oregon writer.

FORESTRY

Old cedars, when the storms come,
hum a fervent anthem
about years, the good life then.

Little trees rustle among
stately trunks that hardly move,
only a slow wind-curtsey.

They hike, the big ones, far
over the pass on good days,
down to a farm's edge at evening.

People walk out and find
the trees discussing religion,
and how to hold your arms when it rains.

—from *My Name Is William Tell*, Confluence Press, 1992

WANT LIST

Bring me the Cascades. Bring that bend
by The Dalles on the Columbia. Over Sherars
Bridge show me the salmon. Put some
sage in the car when we drive to Burns.

When the snows begin, clean off
the windshield with a pine branch
and be sure to carry a thermos of coffee.
Let the far trees bow low.

Then the sound, the long sigh the wind
makes when it passes through leaves.
You stand there waiting for something.
Then a near tree says, "Yes."

—from *The Long Sigh the Wind Makes*, Adrienne Lee Press, 1991

LAKE CHELAN

They call it regional, this relevance—
the deepest place we have: in this pool forms
the model of our land, a lonely one,
responsive to the wind. Everything we own
has brought us here: from here we speak.

The sun stalks among these peaks to sight
the lake down aisles, long like a gun;
a ferryboat, lost by a century, toots
for trappers, the pelt of the mountains
rinsed in the sun and that sound.

Suppose a person far off to whom this lake
occurs: told a problem, he might hear a word
so dark he drowns an instant, and stands dumb
for the centuries of his country and the suave
hills beyond the stranger's sight.

Is this man dumb, then, for whom Chelan lives
in the wilderness? On the street you've seen
someone like a trapper's child pause,
and fill his eyes with some irrelevant flood—
a tide stops him, delayed in his job.

Permissive as a beach, he turns inland,
harks like a fire, glances through the dark
like an animal drinking, and arrives along that line
a lake has found far back in the hills
where what comes finds a brim gravity exactly requires.

—from *Stories that Could Be True:
New and Collected Poems*, Harper & Row, 1977

EVERYONE OUT HERE KNOWS

Flowers jump from the tracks of Big Foot
all over the uplands. In the swamp where
turtles carry their conservative houses
Big Foot waits disguised as a shadow.

The mountains are Big Foot's friends.
They shoulder around. They don't want
too much noise. They report any gunshot
into Big Foot's cave and mutter about it.

Where cliffs are broken, Big Foot was climbing
with its big hands. Rivers that swing wide
are going around mysterious places: you can
stand there and feel the tug of Big Foot's world.

—from *The Long Sigh the Wind Makes*

NIGHT IN OREGON

Pines embraced by their scarves of snow
wait for the sun.
Hemlocks repeat their millions of prayers
bowed down.

Deep in its den a sleepy bear
sucks its paw
where the dream of the forest unfolds in the mountains
on and on.

Out there in a lake a wilderness eye
opens to shine
while stars walk west on their endless hunt
for their perfect home.

Whoever you are, you live in that arch;
you belong,
one of the lost but surrounded by prayer-trees,
all alone.

—from *The Long Sigh the Wind Makes*

A Deeper Calm than Safety

Kim R. Stafford

If wind has a lesson, what is it? If the river says something like words, what are they? If the silence of a rock could by some alchemy be translated into a message, what would we hear? Sunlight streaming down—what does that golden music whisper? And the cold, what few words does the cold clench into the mind?

One time I was driving with my father up the long grade from Burns. At the wheel, I stared steady on. He had folded back his seat, and held his hand over his eyes. I couldn't tell whether he was sleeping. We had been driving all day, which meant several long silences had brought us to new territory in our thinking. Every forty miles, we might come out of our disparate meditations, and make a few remarks. We had crossed the galaxy of Oregon, from the wet crowded throng of the valley to that high, open run of an east Oregon road. My father cleared his throat.

"When I write a poem," my father said, his hand still shading his eyes, "it's like I glimpse something far off—just a little strip of something actual." In the distance, I saw the palisades of a basalt cliff, the columns of stone where the volcano's fire had cooled.

"It's like seeing a strip of the universe," he said, "between the slats of a picket fence. You are passing, and between the pickets you glimpse a little of what's beyond." We were closer to the cliff then, and I could see on its surface the hazy dust of lichen, the dull yellow and sunset smudge where something barely alive held on.

"And then I write another poem," he said, "and I get another glimpse, another strip of light through the fence. And then another, another." The car slowed, labored, crawled. I could see the dark thread of the crack along the vertical edge of each basalt column. A hawk worked the wind deflected upward from the cliff, wings set, still and moving.

"But I never know if the successive glimpses are connected," he said. "Behind the fence, I never know if all those strips of the universe have continuity, a connected substance."

The hawk whirled away at the top of the windshield. We had topped the cliffs. Long strings of parallel cloud loomed up, with furrows of blue between them.

"They're connected," I said. "The strips behind the fence are connected."

"There's no way to tell," he said. We came to the top of Stinking Water Pass. And now I remember our destination: in Boise, he was to appear on a television program about poetry and social issues. I can remember just how they set him up on the night of the program. They had him on a little dais. There was a studio audience of local people, who were supposed to ask questions suggested by the poems. But when the first question turned into a speech about communism, the program loosened up:

Out at our place, when our pigs are suffering from the cold, we go out in the dark and take care of them. In the communist countries, they don't do that, because they don't own those pigs. There's your whole problem right there . . .

Without a question to go on, my father said to the citizen, "Well, I'm not much of an expert about farms, really. My poems are expert, but I'm not." Then he started into a poem. He would read a poem, the camera would close in on his face, and then a series of images would eclipse him—a country road, a grove of trees, a farmhouse:

A telephone line goes cold;
birds tread it wherever it goes.
A farm back of a great plain
tugs an end of the line . . .

On the television screen, my father was replaced by a view of a telephone line with icicles hanging down, then a silhouette of birds flocked against the sky. And music played, a soundtrack I later learned was called "Pastoral Panorama."

"Why do you play music during the poetry?" I asked the producer after the show.

"If we play the music," she said, "everyone is so used to it they won't hear it. If we don't play music, they will miss it."

I stared at her. In the world of the studio, everything followed the logic of the system. But I still had those miles of open country in my head. And I thought about the picket fence. The television left no gaps. You saw it all, heard it all. You couldn't be alone. You could be hurt, but you couldn't hurt on your own. The fabric of sound and image was seamless, coming at you. I thought about the cliff, how the cooling of volcanic fire left gaps between the stone columns. And I knew the discovery in my father's work was not scenic, was not panorama, was not, finally, assurance. His discovery was this: we are alone, we are divided, we die, and we share this predicament. The blank behind each picket makes the strip of light precious. At the farm on the open land—where his parents have died, where the home world of Kansas shut him out, where the chances of his early biography closed:

My self will be the plain,
wise as winter is gray,
pure as cold posts go
pacing toward what I know.

These lines from his early poem "The Farm on the Great Plains" will drive with me on every long road in the dry country. That palisade of basalt, that wind that scratches along the ridge, the hawk that whirls away—glimpsing these were his devotions.

If an empty house had a translator, an advocate, if a lost person had an ambassador, a biographer, if a stretch of country in all its detail of twig and outcrop and rivulet—if all this landscape had some human diplomat, it might be my father. In the poems gathered here, he is the observer of small things:

> Hemlocks repeat their millions of prayers
> bowed down.

He addresses the small things that sum up: it is the habit of the hemlock to decline its highest stem. The forest is a sacred throng. Glance upward, and you will see. But in the poem, you are safe in that outside place, not because you will not suffer, not be lost, not feel cold, not die. You are safe because it's where you should be:

> . . . you belong,
> one of the lost but surrounded by prayer-trees,
> all alone.

You belong, you are accompanied, you are alone. Glimpse, glimpse, glimpse. Each glimpse is true, and successively they dance us in and out of safety: assurance, warning, consolation, ultimatum.

The poems gathered here, and my father's poems generally, do not come to rest in assurance, nor in some final departure from assurance. Instead, as we read them we go back and forth, tasting danger and delight, vinegar and honey, salt and sweet rain, inhaling and exhaling in some kind of existential yoga exercising toward calm. Dawn, storm, sun, dusk, starlight, cold; every sensation is true, and you are privileged to feast on them all.

You are safe, because you have been educated in the world's variety. Yet you know you are not safe, because you recognize the world's terrible variety. Yet you are safe, because you belong in the world's variety, though it buffets you. The trail of your life "is one-person wide."

When my father told me he did not know if his glimpses connected behind the picket fence, I was so afraid that I turned cold. If my father didn't know how all things fit, then maybe they did not. If he could not achieve this principle of coherence, how could I? But now I am assured by his uncertainty. He put his hand over his eyes. He let me drive. He told me what made him afraid. And that was our safety.

Next time I drive that road out beyond Burns, next time the car brings me drifting up toward those stone pickets of the basalt cliff, I know I'll have to pull off and stop. I'll have to turn off the car. The wind comes with a few syllables. The sunlight glimpses me. I stand by the car, and wait. Maybe a bird calls. Maybe not. Or maybe his line comes back: "the long sigh the wind makes." How can I stop myself? I walk through the wind to put my hand against the stone.

WILLIAM STAFFORD, an Oregon resident from 1948 to 1993, was one of the Northwest's most prolific and celebrated poets. His works spanned a range of writing from textbooks to poetry, his primary art form. An author of thirty-five books, Stafford was the recipient of many national honors and was named Oregon Poet Laureate in 1975. He was a lifelong teacher who shared his thoughts with countless students through his thirty years as professor of English at Lewis & Clark College in Portland, and through innumerable workshops and residencies.

◊

In the following short piece, from *My Name is William Tell*, published by Confluence Press in 1992, he writes about being an Oregon artist.

Sniffing the Region

Being tagged a regional artist doesn't hurt that much. Of course the term may imply accomplishment that is worthy only if assessed locally; but being regional may just mean you use references that seem remote and special because the public is elsewhere and hence limited by immersion in a region distinct from the artist's. So artists from another region are distinct—"provincial," even— but without adverse reflection on their accomplishment.

And in a sense any artist has to be regional. Doing art takes a kind of

sniffing along, being steadfastly available to the signals emerging from encounters with the material of the art—the touches, sounds, balancings, phrasings— and the sequential and accumulating results of such encounters.

To look up from the sniffing, in order to find a critic's approval or a public's tastes, is to forsake the trail. And that trail is one-person wide, terribly local and provincial: art is absolutely individual in a non-forensic but utterly unyielding way.

Anyone actually doing art needs to maintain this knack for responding to the immediate, the region; for that's where art is. Its distinction from the academic, the administrative, the mechanical, lies in its leaning away from the past and into the future that is emerging right at the time from the myriadly active, local relations of the artist. Others—administrators, professors, mechanics, or whoever—can of course also be responsive to where they find themselves: —artists have to be. That's the ground for their art, the place where they live.

◊

Stafford was born in Hutchinson, Kansas, in 1914. In a modest résumé, he listed his early work experience in sugar beet fields, construction, an oil refinery, and the United States Forest Service.

He attended college at the University of Kansas, receiving his bachelor's and master's degrees in English. His graduate work during World War II was interrupted by a draft notice. He declared himself a pacifist and a conscientious objector and spent the next four years at camps in Arkansas, Illinois, and California. He later said that the camp experience taught him how it feels to be "different," a notion that carried through his years as a creative writer. His thoughts from C.O. camp formed the manuscript for his first book of prose, *Down in My Heart*, published in 1947.

During the following years, Stafford worked on his doctorate in writing from the University of Iowa. He published poems in national magazines such as *Atlantic Monthly, The New Yorker, The Nation,* and *Harper's.* His first book of poems, *West of Your City,* was published in 1960. He was forty-six years old.

His second book of poems, *Traveling Through the Dark,* received the National Book Award in 1963. In 1970 he was named poetry consultant to the Library of Congress, and he lived in Washington, D.C., for one year. Other major awards included the Shelley Memorial Award of the Poetry Society of America, the Award in Literature from the American Academy and Institute of Arts and Letters, and a Guggenheim Foundation Award. The excellence of his work earned him literature lectureships with the United States Information Service in Western and Eastern Europe, the Middle East, Southeast Asia, India, Pakistan, and Nepal.

Though he appeared soft-spoken and kind, Stafford liked to think of his opinions about life as radical and subversive, often pointing out the responsibility of the artist in this society. As a panelist in a discussion at the Library of Congress, he said that poetry is and should be political, even though it is a creative form; the writer's underlying theory is usually subversive and political because it goes against the mass culture and media. He often declared himself against "officialdom."

Stafford's method was to delve into life as it happened each day. "In everyone's life there is a torrent of things happening," he said. "The writer pays attention to that torrent. The writer doesn't dream of what to write, but what to pick up from that torrent. Crystallizing the thoughts through choice of words, sequencing and cadencing and refining it all are parts of making the final poem."

Stafford always said he wanted to be the kind of person "to whom a lot of things have occurred." Thus, writing for him was not about making a "negotiable poem," one that caught an editor's fancy or would sell for a lot of money. It was about "staying in the current of your life. If that current takes me somewhere else, well, okay.

"I have an appetite for finding the perfect fit of language with the experience of life as you're having it right now. Every now and then you can break off a piece of that and call it a poem."

◇

KIM R. STAFFORD was born in 1949 in Portland, Oregon, where he lives with his daughter. He holds a degree in medieval literature from the University of Oregon and currently directs the Northwest Writing Institute at Lewis & Clark College in Portland.

His published work includes *A Gypsy's History of the World; Braided Apart; The Granary; Rendezvous: Stories, Songs & Opinion of the Idaho Country; Places and Stories; Having Everything Right; Wind on the Waves;* and *We Got Here Together.*